EARN COLLEGE CREDIT FOR WHAT YOU KNOW

SECOND EDITION

EARN COLLEGE CREDIT FOR WHAT YOU KNOW

SECOND EDITION

LOIS LAMDIN

cael

THE COUNCIL FOR ADULT & EXPERIENTIAL LEARNING
CHICAGO

Reprinted 1996

ISBN 0-7872-3039-1

cael

The Council for Adult & Experiential Learning
243 South Wabash Avenue, Suite 800
Chicago, Illinois 60604

All photographs by Victor J.E. Merritt, Visual Images & Concepts; Boston, Massachusetts

Manufactured in the United States of America

To Ezra

*who has helped in more ways than he is aware
and who remains my best "rooter."*

Contents

P

Experience Is The Best Teacher

Since its publication in 1985, *Earn College Credit for What You Know* has helped thousands of adults to understand and prepare for the process of going back to school and turning their non-classroom learning into college credit. The book has been used in prior learning assessment workshops in hundreds of colleges and universities and in employee growth and development programs in major industries and labor unions across the country. Why, then, is The Council for Adult and Experiential Learning (CAEL) putting out a new edition?

A number of changes have taken place in assessment since 1985. New schools have joined the ranks of those which provide or accept prior learning assessment (PLA), and practitioners have extended their techniques and understanding of the assessment process. Testing methods and programs have continued to change and expand. Moreover, as the number of working adults who are going back to school has increased, the variety and types of learnings they present for assessment have broadened and led to consideration of new issues and new practices.

In a rapidly changing economy, recognition of their learning is crucial to most working adults for whom progress on the career ladder is often tied to the acquisition of new skills and competencies. For many people, a significant portion of these new skills and competencies have already been acquired on the job; it is critical that there be ways of measuring, evaluating, documenting and awarding credit for them. One response to this need has been more general acceptance of portfolio-assisted assessment as a flexible way of enabling adults to pull together diverse learnings into a coherent document. There have also been a number of new instruments designed to test technical and professional learnings, and increased importance is being given to evaluation of privately sponsored training programs and recommendation of credit for participation in them.

This second edition of *Earn College Credit for What You Know* has given CAEL an opportunity to respond to some of the questions posed by readers and professionals involved in assessment and to include more information on how adults can manage the shoals and pitfalls of going back to school. New to this edition are a section on career and academic decision making, a consumer's guide to postsecondary education, and a section on how to "survive and thrive" in college. The section on portfolio-assisted assessment has been significantly expanded, and there is new information on testing programs and assessment in technical areas. A state-by-state listing of those colleges and universities which currently have comprehensive assessment programs, based on a recent CAEL national survey, is included in Appendix J.

I am indebted to Susan Simosko, the author of the first edition of *Earn College Credit for What You Know*, for her expertise in all phases of assessment, her ability to make sometimes complicated issues clear and easily understandable, and her enthusiasm for the process and its outcomes. Simosko's work forms the basis for much of this edition, and her contribution to the work is considerable. I hope she understands the admiration and respect I have for her original accomplishment.

Other people have also been crucial to the making of this edition. Primary among them is Mary Fugate, on whom I have relied from the beginning for technical expertise, editorial assistance, professional encouragement, and, above all, friendship. Mary worked with me to develop the outline of the book, and she is responsible for compiling Appendix J. She has proved an invaluable source of practical information about PLA, and she has been on the other end of a phone line for me more times than anyone but the telephone company knows.

And to Morris Keeton, mentor and friend, whose thinking and writing about the philosophical and pragmatic bases of prior learning assessment, whose continuing concern for issues of quality and fairness have provided the foundations on which all of us build, and whose informed editing of the draft manuscript was both meticulous and creative — thank you again.

Special acknowledgment is due to Pat DeWees, whose work on developing strategies to make going back to college easier for adults I have incorporated into chapter 8.

A lot of other people have been helpful and supportive. For whatever is right about this book I must also thank Lynn Schroeder, my editor, whose criticism and suggestions were given, no matter how thorny the issue, cheerfully and with maximum encouragement (she's a great psychologist as well as editor); Urban Whitaker, the quality-assurance maven of assessment, whose ideas lie behind everything I write; Pam Tate, president of CAEL, who invited me to write this book and put CAEL's resources behind it; and the CAEL staff, especially Diana Bamford-Rees and Kris Opas. Staff members were helpful in doing research, collating the results of the College PLA Survey, and, in general, responding when I needed them.

For errors of fact or judgment, I take full responsibility, but then I too am an adult learner, and learning never ends.

I

"One must learn
By doing the thing; for though you
think you know it
You have no certainty, until you try."
—Sophocles

This book is written for the millions of adults in the United States and elsewhere who know that high school graduation is nearer to the beginning of learning than to the end. It is written for all those who have continued to learn and grow since leaving school, those who have developed their job-related skills and competencies or kept up with political events or pursued a sport or craft or hobby or just read and listened and observed and tried new things because they enjoyed knowing more about their world.

This book is being written for you, who had the curiosity to pick it up off a bookstore or library shelf.

Basically the purpose of the book is to help you, the readers, think about what you have learned in your life so far, whether some of that learning may be appropriate for assessment for college credit, and how to go about earning that credit.

This book has three basic aims. The first is to convince you that you are a learner. You have always been a learner. You have been learning since you were first able to grasp a rattle or tie your own shoes or say your first words. You have learned at home and in school, at work and in church, on your own and with the help of parents, friends, spouses, teachers, mentors. You have learned from newspapers and magazines and books, from radio and television, from computers and VCRs, in factories and offices, in museums and churches. You have learned while working in your garden or taking care of your children or managing your neighbor's campaign for city council or rebuilding the engine of your 1965 Pontiac GTO.

The second aim of this book is to help you get credit for those components of your learning that are similar to what is taught in colleges. Everything you have learned is valuable. The sum of your learning is what makes you a competent worker, a caring family member and friend, an informed citizen or a "hot shot" tennis player. But some of what you have learned on your own may also be equivalent to what is being taught in colleges and universities. That is, the knowledge you gained from your job in an automobile plant may approximate what you might have learned in some or all of a program in automotive technology. And the volunteer work you've done with an environmental group, plus your reading on the environment, may have resulted in learnings that are very similar to what is taught in a course on ecology.

You *are* what you have experienced and learned, and everything that you have learned has enriched your life. Acquiring learning on your own is a significant accomplishment that should make you proud. Whether or not some of that learning will prove to be comparable with what is taught in colleges and whether it will also be appropriate to your educational goals or a degree program will be part of your process of discovery as you go through this book and as you talk to assessment advisers in the schools.

Our third aim is to help you to make a successful transition back to school.

The first four chapters of the book will (1) give you an idea of the extent and reasons for the extraordinary movement of adults onto college campuses and how colleges are responding to this movement; (2) present the lifelong learning profiles of five adults who are about to go back to school; (3) encourage you to think about your own goals in seeking further education and to set up an action plan to achieve those goals; and (4) make you a smart consumer of education, so that your choices of schools, programs, courses and activities will reflect your own needs, interests and values.

In chapter 5 you will be looking at all aspects of prior learning assessment: why it is useful to adults, how it works, and, most important, how it can work for you. You will also be encouraged to begin to think about yourself as a learner.

Chapters 6 and 7 will help you find out how to have learning that you have accomplished on your own assessed for college credit, whether through transfer of transcript credit, tests, evaluation of non-college courses taken, or portfolio-assisted assessment.

Finally, chapter 8 addresses some of the issues adults encounter upon returning to school and presents some ideas for devising strategies to cope with these issues.

Throughout the book, you will be encouraged to understand and respect the learning and skills you have acquired. You will also be assisted in defining that learning and those skills in ways that will make it easier to equate them with what is taught in colleges and universities. We will cover the various ways schools go about "assessing" learning and will work on helping you to present the case for the validity of your own learning in the strongest way possible.

Above all, this book should give you respect for yourself as a learner and should deepen the meaning for you of the phrase "Learning never ends."

Earn College Credit for What You Know is written in accord with CAEL's standards of good practice in the assessment of learning for credit (see Appendix A) and is dedicated to helping you receive fair and valid recognition for what you have learned.

1

Going Back to School

Very late in life, when he was studying geometry, someone said to Lacydes, "Is it then a time for you to be learning now?" "If it is not," he replied, "when will it be?"
—*Diogenes*

The Adult on Campus

So you're thinking about going back to school. If you're like most other adults, you're probably also worrying about going back to school. "How will it feel to be the oldest in the class?" "Am I too old to learn?" "Have I forgotten how to study?" "Will the 19-year-olds resent my being there?" "Why am I doing this anyway?" Well, relax. One of the most important trends today is the

One of the most important trends today is the movement of adults like you going back to the campus, and it is transforming the face of higher education across the country.

movement of adults like yourself back to the campus, and it is transforming the face of higher education across the country.

First, more adults are in school today than ever before, and the number is still climbing. You won't be the only one on campus with gray hair and a mortgage or a sink full of dirty dishes waiting for you in the kitchen. Right now, on the average college campus, about two out of five students are combining their studies with working at full-time jobs or caring for young children (or both) and carrying on other family and community responsibilities. More than one-third of college students today are over 25 years old, and in community colleges the average age of students can be as high as 37. On most campuses, adults predominate in evening and weekend classes to the extent that one traditional-age learner apologized to his classmates because he was the only one who wasn't paying his own tuition. This trend, which started about 10 years ago, shows no signs of slackening; a study by the U.S. Department of Education projects that by 1997, 28 percent of all women enrolled in American colleges and universities will be 35 or older. Indeed, if one counts both credit and noncredit enrollments, the head count of adults over the age of 25 already exceeds that of younger students.

The graying of the American population as the nation's average age grows steadily higher, the demands of rapidly changing technologies for trained workers, the average person's realization that there is more to life than a job, beer and television, and the desire to improve the quality of our lives are all factors in the return of adults to the schools that are contributing to dramatic changes on college campuses.

Second, you are not too old to learn. A number of studies confirm that on average, maturity and experience give older students certain advantages over younger students that enable them to more than hold their own academically. Indeed, most college faculty members find that the presence of mature students in their classes is intellectually challenging both to them and to the other students and significantly raises the level of discourse.

And third, if your vision of college is derived from movies in which attractive young people devote most of their energies to football games and dances and spend more time worrying about dates than studying, it's time to update that image. Or if you think college is a place where ancient professors lecture from yellowing pages of notes on boring subjects with no relevance to the real world, that perception also needs revising. The average college campus today is a cosmopolitan place where people of diverse ages, races and ethnic backgrounds pursue their individual academic and career goals in an atmosphere that is increasingly responsive to their varying needs, backgrounds and learning styles.

While most colleges still offer the challenge of competitive sports and the potential for an active social life, those that recognize the changing nature of their students also try to accommodate the needs and interests of part-time adult students who have multiple commitments to jobs, families and economic survival. You are as likely to find a parent-training group as a sorority on campus and to find groups addressing environmental concerns, local traffic, recycling policy, and international peace keeping efforts attended by people of all ages. Professors have grown accustomed to being challenged in class by students who are older than they are, and most of them welcome the interest and commitment of their adult students. If you were to attend the typical college graduation today, you would find in attendance not only parents and grandparents, but also children and grandchildren, proudly watching as their mothers, fathers and grandparents receive diplomas.

Perhaps some of your anxiety about going back to school is based on earlier experiences. If your memories of being in a classroom include boredom, repression, fear of making mistakes or getting bad grades, unsympathetic teachers, too many other students or too many rules, keep in mind that colleges and universities are different from these memories, and, more important, you are different.

Exercise 1-1 provides a way to allow you to think about "then and now," to understand that how you reacted to school when you were a teenager may be very different from how you would react today.

Exercise 1-1: Then & Now

Draw a line down the middle of a piece of paper. On the left side of the line, put down some phrases that represent "then" — how you used to feel about school, the good and the bad. Remember the fun you had with your friends, the trouble you had with algebra or Spanish, your longing to be outdoors playing ball rather than sitting in class, your worries about whether you should wear loafers or sneakers . . . .

On the right side of the line, put down some words or phrases that reflect you "now" — you as an adult who has had a number of significant life experiences and has gained a measure of self-confidence from involvement in work and family and community activities, as an adult who has chosen to go to school. Think about what school can do for you; the level of your adult commitment to learning; your present hopes and fears; the changes in your life that going back to school will create.

Put the piece of paper away for a few days. Then take it out again and, after rereading it, add whatever additional thoughts you have had on either side of the line.

Most adults find that this exercise opens their minds to some profound differences between schooling "then and now" and helps them resolve some of their doubts about returning to the classroom.

What Colleges & Universities are Doing for Adults

Although teaching 18-year-old to 22-year-old traditional students is still an important part of a college or university's job, the adult student represents its future. Institutions of higher education used to "tolerate" adult students; they now welcome them. They used to segregate adults in separate classes, programs or units; they now mainstream them. They used to consider themselves 9-to-5 institutions; they now hold evening and weekend classes. Some of them also provide child care, have special counselors trained to help older students with financial, academic or career issues, offer financial aid packages specifically for adults, encourage adult support groups, and in general are moving toward a more flexible, more individualized way of dealing with the new reality that *ours is a learning society and that all of us are lifelong learners.*

Prior learning assessment programs were to some extent adopted by higher education as a means of attracting older, more experienced men and women. These programs represent recognition that most people are engaged in informal learning activities throughout their lives and come back to the classroom with a background of experiential learning that makes them better students. Colleges have found that if they recognize such learning through fair and reliable evaluation procedures and award college credit when it is deserved, they can enhance the educational experience for their adult students and motivate them to continue learning.

Basic Skills for College Work

Although most adults are better learners than they were in high school, some who didn't get a firm grounding in basic skills during their grade school and high school years — who didn't learn to read, write or do basic mathematical computations with ease —must face the possibility that they may need help in developing these skills before they can progress satisfactorily in college work. If you suspect that your basic skills need improvement, you should face this realistically and find out what kind of support the college of your choice can give you. Most schools offer (or even require) basic skills tests, and they also have special courses, workshops or tutoring programs to help you improve your verbal, mathematic and reasoning skills. Free or low-cost basic skills help is also available to tax payers through local school districts or through the local community college. There is no disgrace in attending these classes or workshops; there *is* disgrace in trying to hide your lack of skills, thereby endangering your ability to succeed in college. You owe it to yourself to eliminate as many barriers to success as possible. Don't stand in your own way.

Learning Styles

Although all of us are learners throughout our lives, our learning styles can be very different. The following story about two brothers illustrates how our learning styles affect how we go about acquiring new knowledge and skills.

After years of living in city apartments, two brothers, Jeff and Sam, moved to a home in the suburbs on a half-acre of land. Both had always wanted a garden, but neither had any experience growing anything beyond a potted philodendron or a scraggly cactus.

Jeff immediately introduced himself to their new next door neighbor, Mr. Ling, whose garden he admired. For the next few months he worked side by side with Mr. Ling, learning what tools he would need, how to prepare the soil, how to plant, when to water and feed, and why mulching is important. He spent long hours in the garden, watching Mr. Ling closely, questioning him about what he didn't understand, and becoming quite skilled in handling the plants. In the fall, Mr. Ling encouraged Jeff to harvest some of his vegetables for himself.

Meanwhile, Sam went about learning to garden in a very different way. He sent away for a number of plant and seed catalogs, which he pored over during the winter to learn the names, habits, and soil and sun requirements of a variety of vegetables and flowers. He also subscribed to a gardening magazine and took a short course on plant diseases at the local agricultural extension college.

By the time spring arrived, Sam had planned their whole garden on paper, sent away for seeds, purchased the tools that were listed as best buys in a consumer's guide and sat back patiently to wait for April. Meanwhile, Jeff had planted tomato, marigold and impatiens seeds in egg-carton containers and had started them under a special light that he installed in the basement.

Jeff looked over Sam's plan and, remembering how clumsy he had felt tiptoeing between the rows in Mr. Ling's garden, suggested that they leave more space in their garden. He also made some changes in the kinds of vegetables they would grow, having observed that root vegetables did not do well in their clay soil.

In late March, when the brothers proudly brought home their first major piece of garden equipment, a roto-tiller, Sam immediately sat down to read the owner's manual, while Jeff tore open the carton and began trying to fit the components together. They both laughed when they realized that once again they were acting out their different learning styles.

Jeff and Sam are both intelligent men, capable of learning complex skills and absorbing a great deal of sophisticated information. But Jeff's preferred learning styles are observation and experimentation. He typically wants to get his hands dirty. Sam's preferred learning styles are reading and reflection. He wants to understand the theory behind something before he tries it out. Together they could really create a terrific garden.

A person's preferred learning style is not necessarily limiting, however. All of us have developed cross-over skills that enable us to learn in a variety of situations: from talking to friends, from watching television, from reading textbooks, from working with machinery, from taking care of a neighbor's baby.

It's a good idea to get to know your own preferred learning styles. It may help you understand why you are more comfortable in the library than in the laboratory or why you like to work on a group project rather than alone. But don't let your learning style preference be a limitation. One of the great things about being a learner is the opportunity it provides not only to increase your knowledge and skills but to broaden the number of ways in which you can learn.[1]

---

1. If you're interested in reading more about learning styles, the following books will be helpful: David A. Kolb, *Learning Style Inventory* (McBer & Co., 1976) and Charles S. Claxton, *Learning Styles* (Washington: American Association for Higher Education, 1978).

Next Steps

Let's assume that you're very comfortable about going back to school. Is it time to fill out an application and register? Perhaps. It's time to apply for admission if:

■ you're fairly clear about why you're going back to school and what you want out of further education;

■ you know which colleges have the courses and programs you need;

■ you have information about how responsive each of those colleges is to adult students;

■ you've thought seriously about what you have learned on your own and about whether that learning may qualify for college credit;

■ you understand the changes in your life style that going back to college may entail.

The balance of this book will help you to think about and understand these issues, to ferret out the information you need, and to make informed decisions that will enable you to fulfill your hope of increasing your potential by returning to learning — whether this means taking a few courses, completing a certificate program or earning a degree.

2

Profiles of Five Adult Learners

"Only so much do I know, as I have lived."
—*Ralph Waldo Emerson*

In the five case histories that follow, you will get to know some actual adult learners, all of them interesting people who may be similar to people you know — or even to you. These men and women come from different backgrounds, have lived very different lives, and have developed diverse interests, skills and learnings. What they have in common is that they have reached a crucial point in their lives, a point when further education makes sense if they are to move on in their personal lives and in their careers.

In later chapters, we will refer to these people and look at how they approached and resolved many of the decisions you will be facing as you contemplate going back to school. And you will discover how Scott, Joan, Dorene, Max and Anna chose career paths, schools, and programs and went about preparing to have their prior learning assessed for college credit.

Scott A.

Scott A. is 46 years old. Since he was 16 he has worked at various jobs for a paper company. He has planted trees, cut timber, transported it down the river, and done a number of other jobs, both skilled and nonskilled, that are part of logging. He is also a good mechanic and is the one everyone turns to when a tractor or skidder or giant saw malfunctions.

Thinking that he might like a change, Scott spent a few years on transfer to the company's paper mill in a nearby city. While he learned a lot about the technology of paper making, that experience taught him that he would be miserable if he had to spend all his working days cooped up in a factory. He needs the feeling of freedom he gets from working outdoors.

Scott never graduated from high school. This began to bother him when his own children reached high school, so two years ago he started to attend evening school to study for a G.E.D. (general education development exam; the G.E.D. is equivalent to a high school diploma). He passed the test easily, and his experience has given him the courage to think about going on to college.

For the past few years, Scott has worked as first assistant to Rich, a unit manager with a degree in forestry. Rich has encouraged Scott to take advantage of the company's prepaid tuition plan to go back to school so that he can advance into a crew leader position. This prospect appeals to Scott because he no longer feels as strong or agile as he once was, and his present job involves physical risk. Scott sometimes thinks about early retirement, but he would need to earn money to supplement his reduced pension and has begun to think about alternative careers.

In his leisure time, Scott does a lot of bass fishing. He also belongs to a Bible study group and is an accomplished wood worker who has designed and made much of the furniture in his home.

Scott is 46 years old and works for a large lumber company. He has become both a skilled mechanic and an accomplished wood worker.

Scott has already made initial inquiries about local educational opportunities and has found a community college that not only offers an associate degree in forestry but will assess his prior learning for possible credit.

Joan B.

Joan B. grew up in a large city in the East, spending much of her time during high school cutting classes so that she could visit museums and galleries and see the latest foreign films. Although she learned a lot about art, her school grades were low and she could get into only a "second rate" college, which she left after the first semester.

Against her family's wishes, Joan married when she was 19 and had two children by the time she was 21. Because her husband was fairly well to do, she didn't work outside her home. Later she trained to become a volunteer docent (guide) at the local art museum, worked with the city's committee to build an arts center, and teamed up with a friend to write, direct and produce a film on artists in the city.

Joan's husband became an alcoholic, and, when drunk, a wife abuser. Although she spent many years trying to help him by supporting his involvement in Al Anon and other counseling programs, Joan finally left him when his addiction worsened and he began to abuse the children. Although Joan receives some child support for her 15- and 17-year-old sons, she gets no money for herself. Her long-range plans are to earn a graduate degree in business so she can pursue a career as an administrator of arts programs. Her immediate goal is to complete the college degree she began 18 years ago.

A local college has a prior learning assessment program, and Joan is beginning to think about what college-level learning she has acquired on her own.

Joan is a 42-year-old divorced mother of two children. After years of experience as a volunteer at a local art museum, her short term goal is to complete the college degree in art she began 18 years ago.

Dorene G.

Dorene G. went straight from high school into a secretarial job with a major communications company. She learned typing, filing and shorthand in her high school vocational education program, and since joining the company has become proficient in using computers, has taken a company course in a computerized spreadsheet program and has taught herself word processing. She is the office expert in word processing and is responsible for teaching the program to new secretaries. She has also taught herself desktop publishing and has designed and produced on her own the new company personnel forms and a personnel benefits brochure. She was very proud when the president told her supervisor that Dorene had done a better job than the professional designer who had prepared the previous brochure.

In the past, Dorene was closely affiliated with her union and was active in organizing and contract arbitration. She has taken a number of union-sponsored courses in labor relations and labor history.

Because the grandparents who raised Dorene were born in Puerto Rico, she grew up speaking English and Spanish. She has made a few trips to Puerto Rico to visit relatives and has become politically involved in the Puerto Rican movement for statehood, on which she has read a great deal and for which she gives speeches and writes articles. She also reads fiction by Puerto Rican and other Latin American authors in the original Spanish and collects native South American crafts.

Dorene's ambition is to move up to a management position in the company, but she believes she needs further credentials. She would like to take advanced work in computer science, but she hesitates to commit herself to going for a degree at this time because she hopes to get married and have children in a few years. She also doesn't want to take courses in subjects she thinks she already knows, which is why she is investigating the possibility of prior learning assessment.

Dorene, now 27 years old, went straight from high school into a secretarial position, where she eventually became proficient in office skills and several computer software applications.

Max W.

Max W. works for a major automobile manufacturer, where he manages the parts warehouse in a truck division. Prior to being trained by the company for that job, he had worked on the production line doing welding, painting and assembly. During the Vietnam War he spent two years in the U.S. Coast Guard, where he was in charge of communications for his company.

Max is a single parent, raising two small children by himself, and in his spare time he and his girlfriend are active in a black community youth group working with troubled school dropouts. He also plays the trumpet and is interested in both jazz and classical music.

Max's company provides support for going back to school, and Max says, "It's my time now." He finished a CLEP preparation course and then took five general CLEP tests, a widely accepted program that tests college-level learning, for which he was awarded 30 credits toward an associate's degree. Before committing himself to a college program, he wants to get a rough picture of how much additional credit he might be able to earn through prior learning assessment.

Anna P.

Until her recent fiftieth birthday, Anna never wanted to be anything but a wife and mother. She married her childhood sweetheart right after high school and had four children. While they were growing up, she became interested in child psychology and child development. Anna read many books on the subject and attended courses on parenting and child care at her church and through the continuing education classes at her local high school. After her mother died of cancer, she also became active in the local cancer society, running their fund-raising campaign for three consecutive years. During that time she was responsible for recruiting part-time volunteers, scheduling and managing their time, assigning their duties, and planning and coordinating all of the group's activities.

Max, a 35-year-old single parent of two young children, works for a major automobile manufacturer as manager of the parts warehouse. In his spare time, he is active in a community youth group for troubled school dropouts.

Anna's leisure time pursuits include gourmet cooking and baking, for which she is locally well known. She is frequently asked to help cater church and community events and has taken a number of noncredit courses in Chinese, French and Near Eastern cooking.

Anna reads a great deal, mostly novels by such nineteenth century authors as Charles Dickens, Anthony Trollope, and George Eliot. She has also read biographies of these authors and has begun to branch out into reading critical studies of their work.

Now that her children are either away at college or preparing for it, Anna is wondering what she wants to do with the rest of her life. A friend suggested that she might start a catering business, but Anna is worried about her lack of business experience. She is thinking about going to college for a business degree, but can't imagine spending the next four years doing that on a full-time basis. She wonders if there is any way to shorten the time needed for a bachelor's degree.

The Value of Prior Learning Assessment

All five of these people are at a stage of life in which a change of some sort is in process or is anticipated. Scott wants to position himself to get a better job in his company now, but he is also looking forward to developing skills that will let him earn a living if he takes early retirement. Joan needs to turn her volunteer activities into a paid career so that she can support her family. Dorene wants to move from a secretarial to a management position. Max wants to go to school to become a more rounded, better educated person. ("It's my time now.") And Anna finds that as her full-time job as a mother is coming to an end, it's time to broaden her horizons beyond home and family.

For all five of these people, further schooling seems to be a point of entry for moving on to the next phase of their lives. And all five have already accumulated at least some learning that may be similar to that which they could have acquired in a college setting.

Anna, who recently turned 50, studied a great deal about child psychology and child development while raising her four children. While at home, she also became a gourmet cook, for which she has become well known in her community.

For Scott, Dorene, Joan, Max and Anna, prior learning assessment will:

- validate the worth of learning they have achieved on their own;
- demonstrate to them what they still need to learn in order to achieve their personal, career or academic goals;
- shorten the time necessary to earn a college degree;
- save them money by lessening the number of courses they need to take;
- enhance their pride and self-esteem for what they have accomplished as learners; and
- make them aware that learning is truly a lifelong process.

3

Life & Career Planning

Making Informed Decisions

> *"All experience is an arch
> to build upon."*
> —Henry Adams

The purpose of this chapter is to help you think about your life, career, and academic goals in the context of a rational and realistic career-planning process; to engage you in some self-assessment exercises that will help you understand your own values, interests and skills; and to introduce you to the career-planning resources in your community.

The Importance of Life & Career Planning

Why, you may be wondering, is there a chapter on life and career planning in a book on prior learning assessment? What does this have to do with me and my desire to earn college credit?

There are a number of connections to be made between prior learning assessment and life and career planning. For one, you must be able to look at your prior learning in the context of what you plan to study in college. Some components of your prior learning may be more relevant to your educational goals than others, and you will want to emphasize these. For example, if you plan to enter a four-year program in social work, the knowledge you gained as a child-care worker will be more closely related to your major than your ability to install telephone systems. Or, if you plan to work toward a degree in computer science, you will put more emphasis on your experience in computer programming than on your skills in fashion merchandising.[1] In any case, you have to demonstrate to your assessors the connections between your prior learning and what you wish to study.

To put it another way, although the learning you hope to have assessed took place in the past, your reasons for assessment should be directed toward your future. If you are able to state your life goals explicitly, you will be better able to make specific educational plans (including plans for prior learning assessment) to reach those goals.

Even if you think you are certain of why you are going back to school and what you plan to study there, you still might take some time to at least skim this chapter to see if any of its content applies to you. Situations change, the economy changes, our personal likes and dislikes change. Even if you have been through some life-planning exercises before, you will probably find it worthwhile to think about some of the issues raised in the following pages, to complete some of the self-assessment exercises, and to attempt to set down on paper your specific reasons for wanting to go back to school.

---

1. Your learnings in fields other than your major (or concentration) may still be useful in fulfilling your elective (or general distribution) requirements.

What do you want to be doing in five years? Ten years? Do you want to enter a new vocation or profession? Do you want to increase your competence in a skill you already have? Do you want to find a solution to a serious social or environmental problem? Do you want to enrich your retirement years? Do you want to acquire credentials for professional advancement? Do you want to change your routine and learn something entirely new? Answering these and other questions about your future will help you map out your educational objectives and will also assist you in thinking about the learning you have already accomplished.

Exercise 3-1 will help you begin to define exactly why you're contemplating going back to school, what you hope to get out of it, and how to think about the issues of courses, programs and degrees as they relate to your current job and future career or life goals.

Defining Your Career Goals

Perhaps you are already very clear about your career goals. You may want to earn a certificate in paralegal studies so that you can move up from secretary in your present legal firm to a better paying, more professional position in that same firm. Or you may be planning to take a few courses in bookkeeping and business skills so you can get out of your present job selling cars and open a motorcycle repair shop with your brother-in-law. Or your plans may be to earn a bachelor's degree in agronomy as a first step toward getting a job in the U.S. Department of Agriculture. Or you may just want to take some writing courses so you can write your family's history.

It is important to understand that career planning does not necessarily mean career change. If you are happy or secure in your present job, you may or may not wish to change that job for another, even within the same organization. On the other hand, if your current job leaves you feeling unfulfilled or like a square peg in a round hole, you may wish to move on to something totally different or to develop a "second career" or hobby that will give

There are a number of resources available to help you get the information you need as you go through the process of career planning.

Exercise 3-1: Why Do You Want to Go Back to School?

Take a few minutes to think about this question; then write a brief statement about why you want to go to school. Be as specific as possible about your needs and interests and the decisions you have already made. The point of stating, as specifically as possible, your reasons for going back to school is to enable you to make intelligent, informed choices about your future: which school to attend, which programs or courses to take, whether it is in your interest to work toward a degree, and so forth. Your first statement may be general, such as "I want to improve my job skills," or "I want to become a graphic artist," or "I want to help people," but if it is going to help you, you must try to refine it.

For example, Dorene G. (see her profile, Chapter 2, p. 16), who works in an office where she uses the computer for word processing and spreadsheets, wants to go to school to "learn more about computers." That's a fine beginning statement, but before it can serve as a guide to further choices, Dorene needs to think about some of the following:

- Does she want to "learn more about computers" to do something specific like using a database management system?

- Is she interested in computers from the perspective of an engineer (how they work, how they are designed), a sociologist (what is the computer's effect on society), or a public health specialist (what are the risks of prolonged exposure to a video display terminal)?

- Since she is hoping to advance to a management position in her present company, would it be to her advantage to earn a degree? If so, which degree?

- Would a certificate program in computer science or computer programming or management information science (MIS) answer her needs as well as would a degree?

→

27

> ■ If her needs are specific, such as wanting to learn desk-top publishing or spreadsheet analysis, could one or two courses give her the skills and information she wants?
>
> These are the kinds of questions Dorene should ask herself before she tries to make final choices about schools, programs or courses.
>
> *What kinds of questions do you need to ask yourself that will enable you to make smart choices?* It may be that you aren't able to be more specific at this time because you need more information or more time to think about it. You may even feel that you need to talk to a guidance counselor who can help you make decisions about your career and academic goals. That's OK. In fact, knowing that you don't know enough to make a good decision right now may be the most helpful outcome of this exercise. It may spur you on to get the information you need.

you more personal satisfaction. In that case, you should be aware that every organization has career paths, opportunities to move sideways to very different jobs or upward to more complex or more responsible jobs in the same general area. These paths are not always well publicized or clearly articulated, so you may have to piece information together from several sources to understand how they work. Just remember that you don't always have to switch companies in order to switch jobs.

To make informed decisions about your own career path, you should not only learn more about career opportunities that relate to your current job or to the field you want to study, you should listen to the inner voice that tells you what values and interests you must satisfy if you are to be happy in your work life.

Values Assessment

We are all different. June enjoys selling major kitchen appliances at the Acme Home Store. She enjoys meeting customers and discovering the best way to get and keep their interest. She enjoys learning about the technical aspects of her merchandise. She even enjoys the competition with other salespeople in the store. Her best friend, Sherie, is much happier working in the back office at Acme. Sherie is uncomfortable with strangers, is not interested in technical information and hates competition. She also feels that she lacks the stamina to stand on her feet on the sales floor all day long, and she doesn't want to work on Saturdays when her children are home from school. On the other hand, Sherie enjoys laying out Acme's newspaper ads, likes setting up business systems, and takes pride in her knowledge that she writes better business letters than anyone else in the firm.

Although both June and Sherie seem well matched for their current jobs, June's ambitions for more money and increased prestige have made her consider earning a degree in retailing. This will enable her to build on her present skills and put her in line for a career as buyer or sales manager. Ultimately, June hopes to own her own store, so she also wants to develop some business and financial management skills.

Sherie, on the other hand, cares less about money than she does about having more leisure time to spend with her children and to work on her part-time job, illustrating children's books. Her goal is to find a career that will enable her to work at home while pursuing her artistic interests. This fall she plans to take a course in child development to enhance her parenting skills and a drawing workshop given by a well-known illustrator to develop her creative talents. She hopes eventually to leave her present job and work full time at home as an illustrator.

Both women have become aware that their own values and interests are as important as their skills in determining their futures, and they are making their educational plans accordingly.

Exercise 3-2 provides an opportunity for you to begin thinking about your own values — what's really important to you — and about how those values are now or can be expressed in the work you do.

Once you have begun to think seriously about your own values, you will take them into consideration whenever you are

Exercise 3-2: Assessing Your Values

Following is a list of values for you to consider. Some values will be more important to you than others. Some may not be very important at all. Rank these values from most important (1) to least important (16).

To rank the values, imagine you have the world's worst job where none of your values are fulfilled. If your employer offered you a chance to have one of your values fulfilled, which one would it be? What would be the next one? The next? Keep going until you have ranked all 16. Expect to change your mind several times before coming up with your final order. (Put the numbers in the left margin, and use a pencil so you can erase when you change your mind.)

Ranking Your Values

_____ Advancement: A chance to advance in a career; to be promoted.

_____ Learning: A chance to learn new skills and knowledge.

_____ Money: Having a decent salary and benefits; a chance for overtime.

_____ Recognition: Having your efforts appreciated; getting credit for a job well done; having your suggestions considered seriously.

_____ Working Conditions: Having a pleasant work environment (not too hot, cold, dirty, noisy, crowded).

_____ Relationships: Having a good working rapport with your supervisor and co-workers; team spirit; companionship.

_____ Hours: Having the work schedule you want (daytime, nighttime, weekdays, weekends, full time, part time).   →

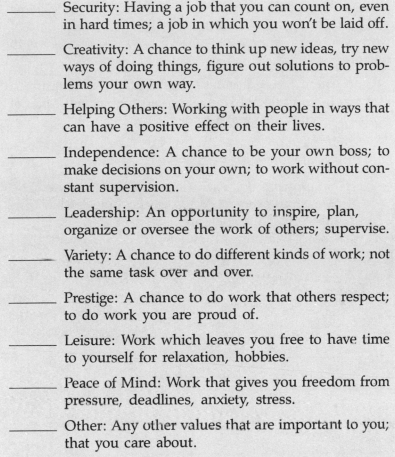

_____ Security: Having a job that you can count on, even in hard times; a job in which you won't be laid off.

_____ Creativity: A chance to think up new ideas, try new ways of doing things, figure out solutions to problems your own way.

_____ Helping Others: Working with people in ways that can have a positive effect on their lives.

_____ Independence: A chance to be your own boss; to make decisions on your own; to work without constant supervision.

_____ Leadership: An opportunity to inspire, plan, organize or oversee the work of others; supervise.

_____ Variety: A chance to do different kinds of work; not the same task over and over.

_____ Prestige: A chance to do work that others respect; to do work you are proud of.

_____ Leisure: Work which leaves you free to have time to yourself for relaxation, hobbies.

_____ Peace of Mind: Work that gives you freedom from pressure, deadlines, anxiety, stress.

_____ Other: Any other values that are important to you; that you care about.

Based on your own numbering of this list, rank your values in order of importance on the worksheet starting on the next page (most important near the top; less important near the bottom). Next to each value, indicate how satisfied or how dissatisfied you are with respect to it in your present job and what you hope for in your next job. To fill out the third column, think about your critical values, those that must be present for you to accept a job. The classic example is the person who can only work out of doors and will not accept office work no matter how high the salary or great the

→

prestige. Can you imagine a kind of work that would allow you to express your own unique values? Is that the kind of work you are planning to study for when you return to school?

If your expressed values seem far from your anticipated life's work, you may wish to talk to a career or educational counselor before making further decisions.

Ranking Scale for Values Exercise

0 No problem. I am satisfied with things as they are.
1 Some improvement would be nice, but I can live with things the way they are.
2 I don't like things they way they are. I want to do something about it.
3 I am very dissatisfied. I definitely want a change.

Rank	Value	Present Job	Next Job
1.			
2.			
3.			
4.			
5.			
6.			
7.			
8.			
9.			

→

10. _____

11. _____

12. _____

13. _____

14. _____

15. _____

16. _____

Note that the values at the top of the list are the most important to you. If some of them received a score of 2 or 3, you may want to consider holding out for greater satisfaction in these critical areas in your next job.

confronted with the need to make career choices or other life-style choices. Perhaps you have found that money is less important to you than your working conditions, or that you are willing to trade off prestige for peace of mind. These are critical issues that can lead to long term satisfaction or dissatisfaction with your career, so don't ignore them. And don't discount the possibility that these values may change; they can shift depending upon your age and new interests. Some counselors recommend that people repeat a values exercise every few years to keep in touch with changes in their own needs.

Skills Assessment

Skills are the things you do well, things for which you have talent or that you have learned to do. They may be related to your present job (typing, fixing machinery, selling, teaching) or they may be unrelated to it (entertaining, playing basketball, working with teenagers, singing). Most people possess 500–700 specific skills, most of which are marketable, so don't be modest about your own list. Put down as many skills as you can think of.

It may be helpful to think about your skills in terms of the following categories (see also the general skills list in Appendix C):

Communications
> Reading
> Writing
> Speaking
> Listening

Mathematical/Computational

Intellectual
> Ability to learn
> Analysis
> Synthesis
> Critical reasoning
> Scientific reasoning
> Problem solving

Interpersonal
> Ability to get along with different kinds of people
> Leadership
> Negotiation
> Teamwork/working in groups
> Influencing

Physical
> Specific sports skills
> Specific physical abilities

Personal
> Creativity
> Self-development
> Persistence
> Motivation
> Planning
> Self-confidence

Professional or technical
> Skills that enable one to do specific jobs — build things, fix things, manage things, etc.

A skills list was compiled by Scott, the man who works in the timber industry (see profiles, chapter 2, pp. 12–14). His list is not complete, but he has made a good start at determining what skills he has already acquired in life.

Communications:
> Reading comprehension (Scott enjoys reading the Bible, Bible commentary, mysteries, sports articles and books)
>
> Speaking (He leads a Bible study group, makes speeches to local organizations in support of sports for kids)
>
> Listening (to facilitate discussion in the Bible study group, he must listen intently to what people say in order to respond appropriately)

Mathematical/computational
> Arithmetic
>
> Algebra and plane geometry
>
> Figuring board-feet of lumber

Interpersonal
> Gets along well with logging manager and fellow workers
>
> Is the one in the family to whom his brothers bring their problems
>
> Has sustained a happy marriage for 12 years
>
> Still close to old friends from high school

Physical
> Fishing
>
> Bowling
>
> Weight lifting

Professional or technical
> Wood-working
>> Finishing/refinishing
>>
>> Basic carpentry
>>
>> Furniture design
>>
>> Furniture making
>
> Mechanical
>> Maintaining diesel engines, heavy machinery, boat motors

Applied electronics
Fixing electric appliances, wiring, re-wiring
Forestry
Timbering, transporting
Operating bull dozers, tractors, skidders
Re-foresting (planning/planting)

Once his counselor convinced Scott that he was not "bragging," he was able to extend the list far beyond what you see above, particularly in such areas as leadership, persistence, motivation and self-development.

Anna (see profiles, chapter 2 pp. 15, 20), who is rather shy, had to be persuaded by a college counselor to even attempt listing her skills. Her initial list is quite different from Scott's, but also extensive.

Communications
Reading (Anna has read extensively in child psychology and nineteenth-century British fiction; she also reads two newspapers a day and subscribes to a number of cooking magazines)
Listening (Anna says a good parent must know how to listen carefully)
Speaking German (Anna's parents were refugees from Germany in World War II, and she learned the language to communicate better with them and other relatives)
Mathematical/computational
Household budgeting
Conversion of recipe ingredients from metric to U.S. measures, equivalents
Interpersonal
Child care, child psychology
Making and keeping friends
Entertaining
Maintaining a happy, loving marriage
Physical
Aerobic dancing
Hiking

Professional or technical
    Basic cooking techniques
    Basic baking techniques
    Other cuisines (German, French, Chinese, Near
        Eastern)
    Catering
    Household management
    Management of a nonprofit organization
    Planning
    Personnel management
    Administration

Exercise 3-3: Your Skills

List your own skills on a separate piece of paper. Do you use any of your skills in your present job? How could you use your strongest skills more? Are there any skill areas you'd like to develop more?

Remember, many of your skills are *transferable*, that is, they can be used with some modification in different situations. If you have shown an aptitude for simple arithmetic in your current job as a bookkeeper, you may find that you do well in other aspects of mathematics, in engineering, and possibly in science. Or if you are a competent truck driver with a "feel" for engines, you may do well in physics, mechanics or engineering. Basic language skills — speaking, reading, writing, listening — are highly transferable in fields as diverse as selling, business management, journalism, and teaching. Homemaking skills may translate well to hospitality management, social work, dressmaking or child care. In any case, your skills go with you through life and can greatly ease the transition from one mode of work to another.

Certainly, many of these skills will directly influence how well you do in further schooling. Whether they are appropriate for credit or not, they will make you a better learner and facilitate your success in college.

Resources for Career Planning

Once you have formed some idea of your own interests, values and skills, you are better equipped to determine what kinds of work might capitalize on your strengths, fulfill your needs, and enable you to earn a better living. In a constantly changing labor market, you will also need information about the current availability of jobs in your area as well as the educational and experiential requirements for those jobs. There are a number of resources available to help you get the information you need as you go through the process of career planning:

1. Counselors at your local high school, the public library or the college you are planning to attend.

2. Computerized career information systems such as SIGI-PLUS or Discover for Adults (these also may be available at high schools, public libraries and colleges).

3. Career counselors in the personnel department of your company or union.

4. Informational interviews with people holding the kinds of jobs in which you might be interested.

5. A computer database, Guidance Information Services (GIS), available in many schools and employment services, which has up-to-date information on the job outlook for different careers.

6. The *Dictionary of Occupational Titles* (DOT), available in most libraries. It is a classification of most jobs that exist in the United States. The jobs are described in detail, and they are classified with groups of related jobs. The *Occupational Outlook* discusses the educational requirements and job outlook for almost as many jobs. The two books are cross-referenced so that they can be used together.

7. Books on the job market and on different careers in your geographic area; these forecasts are often published by the Department of Commerce in your own state. A librarian can help you find the best sources for information on any career-related subject.

8. Professional journals with recent articles about the field. Almost every occupation has its own trade or professional journal. If you take the time to look through the journals of some of the career fields that interest you, you can learn a lot about future trends in those careers.

A creative way of going about the process of making career decisions is to read social trends. The following seem to be well-established trends in the United States:

- the population is aging;
- two-earner families are becoming the norm;
- computers are becoming more common in the home; and
- the population is more health conscious.

Think about these trends for a few minutes. What social changes might they involve? What goods and services might older people and families with two incomes need? Does the increasing number of home computers suggest any new or expanded opportunities for jobs? Does the expansion of health services suggest any new career opportunities?

For example, both older people and working women are increasingly turning to fast foods or catered meals, creating a number of new jobs in the food industry. An older population combined with the expanded health consciousness of Americans is a strong factor in the growth of health-related industries. And the increasing availability of computers (as well as telephone-answering machines and fax machines) has enabled thousands of people to carry on their work in their homes. These and many trends like them will have a dramatic impact on the kinds of jobs that will be available in this country over the next decade. They demand that you do some creative thinking about what opportunities may open up for you.

Developing Your Own Action Plan

Your future isn't something that just happens to you. You can make it what you want it to be. But this takes planning. If you have read through this chapter and done the exercises, you should be ready to begin right now shaping your own future. What you need is a plan, a plan designed by you, for you — that will keep you on track to get where you want to go. Exercise 3-4 will help you formulate such a plan.

Exercise 3-4: Your Own Action Plan

On a separate piece of paper, prepare your own action plan, using the format below as a model. Tape your plan above your desk, or put it in a safe place where you will see it every-day. Then start to put it into action.

1. Name:

2. My current career goals are (be as specific as you can):

   Short Term:

   Long Term:

3. I need the following preparation for this career:

   (This may include courses, degrees, licenses, cer-tificates, union membership, experience, any re-quirements necessary to make yourself eligible for employment in the career of your choice)

4. My skills/interests:

   a. Job skills:

   b. Talents and aptitudes:

   c. Interests:

5. My current education goals: (e.g., enrolling in

   _____ school; doing independent study at

   _____ ; other _____).

   →

Short term:

Long term:

6. Action plan (steps to achieve your career and education goals):

a. _____

b. _____

c. _____

d. _____

e. _____

f. _____

7. Actions to take immediately: (e.g. finding out if the local college offers the specific program you need, writing for a transcript, talking to a career counselor, getting information about prior learning assessment at the University, applying for admission, enrolling for a course, etc.)

8. Actions to take within the next three months:

9. Timeline: (Do a week-by-week, month-by-month, year-by-year outline of what you will do to accomplish your goals.)

10. Pledge: I will carry out this action plan to the best of my ability in order to achieve my own career/educational objectives.

Signed: _____

Your action plan will be especially useful to you when planning your college program or thinking about career change. Be sure to take it with you when you have scheduled a meeting with your college advisor or counselor.

A First Step

This chapter has been only an introduction to career planning, a first step in the process. The intention is to encourage you to think about your future creatively, to make some preliminary decisions, to define your goals and find out what you need to do to achieve those goals, and to set about translating goals into reality. Appendix B contains a list of books and other resources useful for career planning.

4

Choosing the Right School

A Consumer's Guide to Postsecondary Education

"Where there is much desire to learn, there of necessity will be much arguing, much writing, many opinions; for opinion in good men is but knowledge in the making."
—*John Milton*

By now you've thought about why you want to go to school and what you want to study, you've developed an action plan, and you're ready to begin. Right? Well, not quite. There are very important differences among schools, and choosing the one that is accessible to you and right for you is not always easy. You wouldn't buy a car or a washing machine without doing some research on which is the best model (and the best buy) for your needs, nor would you go on a vacation without finding out whether the sports activities you like are available, what the weather is likely to be, and how much it will cost in both time and money.

In some ways, choosing a school is similar to choosing a car, a washing machine or a vacation spot; the more you know about the alternatives, the better chance you have of making a choice that will be right for you. The point of this chapter is to help you become a smart consumer of postsecondary education, to learn how to identify the college or other kind of school that is right for you and that will meet your needs in terms of degrees offered, programs and courses available, schedule, accessibility, services, and so forth. The following pages cover:

- the way colleges and universities work;
- their special vocabulary (some people call it jargon);
- the advantages of degree and nondegree study;
- nontraditional alternatives;
- the kinds of questions you should ask about the schools you are considering;
- the nature of your own demands on a school, both negotiable and nonnegotiable;
- the way to find the information you need to make intelligent decisions; and
- the way to "hedge your bets."

Musts & Wants

Let's begin by thinking about what is most important to you in a school. Exercise 4-1 will help you define what you must demand of a college. It lists some of the important things adults look for when they're thinking of going back to the classroom. As you go down the list, look at each item in terms of its relative importance to you. The *"musts"* are qualities that are critical in making it possible to go back to school; the *"wants"* are desirable and will certainly make it easier; the *"don't cares"* aren't important to you. For example, if you are a single parent with no friends or family living nearby who can help take care of your child and have no means of paying a babysitter, then a campus child-care center is a must. If you already have a good babysitter but think it would be more convenient to have your child in a nursery school on campus, that would be a want. But if you have no children, have children but also have a convenient childcare arrangement, or have children who are grown, then you probably don't care whether there is a child-care center on campus.

In exercise 4-1, some possible wants and needs are suggested, but don't limit yourself to these items. Add your own list of expectations and then check off the appropriate column.

Exercise 4-1: Musts & Wants

Item	Must Have	Want	Don't Care
A special program in			
_____	_____	_____	_____
A strong department of			
_____	_____	_____	_____
A college within _____ miles of home or work	_____		
Late afternoon or evening child-care service	_____		
Bus or train service to campus	_____		
Free parking on campus	_____		
All required courses offered after 5:00 P.M.	_____		

→

School calendar: flexible?
convenient? realistic? _____

Availability of independent
study, telecourses, etc. _____

Library open on Sundays _____

Prior learning assessment
program available:
    CLEP exams?
    ACE evaluation of
      military and
      corporate courses?
    Portfolio assessment? _____

Other (fill in your
specific needs) _____

    Keep your musts and wants in mind as you go through the following material, remembering that even the "best" schools are good for you only if they offer what you need.

How Schools & Colleges Work

If you wish to become a smart consumer of higher education, you should be able to "speak college"; that is, you should understand terms such as *semester* and *credit hour*; know the difference between degree and nondegree study; and, in general, be able to make decisions about your own schooling based on a solid understanding of what is and is not available, possible or desirable for you. (For quick reference to the meaning of unfamiliar terms used here or elsewhere, see the glossary.)

There are many kinds of postsecondary schools and colleges in the United States that fulfill different needs. Some of these are listed below.

Two-year or community colleges. These are closely related to the communities supporting them. They offer associate of arts (A.A.), associate of science (A.S.) or associate of applied science (A.A.S.) degrees as well as noncredit courses covering a large range of vocational, technical and academic subjects. Most community colleges have a high percentage of part-time adult students and offer many of their classes and services at hours convenient to working people.

Community colleges usually have arrangements for transferring credits earned there to four-year colleges, but special conditions sometimes apply to certificate or A.A.S. programs. Students should check on these special conditions prior to entering programs from which they hope to transfer.

Because they are state and locally supported, community colleges are usually less expensive than other colleges.

Colleges. These offer bachelor's degrees (four years of full-time study, considerably more to complete a degree on a part-time basis) in liberal arts and sciences as well as in some vocational/professional areas. Most colleges also offer some continuing education and adult weekend or evening courses and programs. Colleges differ widely in their percentage of residential and nonresidential students, in their emphasis on the purely academic versus vocational/technical subjects, and in their desire to attract and serve adults.

Universities. These are usually made up of a collection of graduate and professional schools that offer master's degrees and doctorates and an undergraduate division that awards bachelor's degrees. In general, their admissions standards tend to be higher, and most put emphasis on research as well as teaching.

To accommodate their adult students, most universities have evening and/or weekend classes as well as a noncredit continuing education division.

Proprietary Schools. These are privately owned, for-profit schools that usually focus on one or more technological or vocational areas, such as electronics, computers or paralegal studies. In most states they must be licensed, and in some states they are permitted to award degrees as well as certificates. Caution should be exercised regarding the transferability of credit to other institutions.

Adult community-based schools. These are typically sponsored by local school districts, churches, labor unions, YMCAs, women's groups and other community organizations. Courses typically cover a wide range of subjects and are designed to serve the needs of the sponsoring organization's constituencies. The courses are of varying length and intellectual depth. They tend to focus on practical and cultural subjects or on current issues. They do not carry credit.

Vocational/Technical Schools. These may be state or local community sponsored and may have transfer arrangements with the local high schools or community colleges. They train people for specific trades or occupations.

As you can see, there is a wide variety of schools, each serving somewhat different needs and constituencies. If you want to get a two-year degree in a technical area such as automotive technology or commercial art, you will want to look closely at your local community college to see if it offers the desired program. And if you want eventually to teach junior high school science, you will look to a four-year college that offers degrees in education or a university that offers the possibility of going on to graduate study. But if you want to learn a trade such as electronics or a practical skill such as welding, you will probably want to investigate your local community college, vo-tech schools and proprietaries to compare their programs and determine how long the course of study is, what it costs, and how much help each institution will give you in finding a job.

Joan B's (see profile, chapter 2, p. 14) search for an appropriate school is a case in point. Joan's immediate goal is to get a bachelor of arts degree in art history with the eventual goal of going on to a graduate school of business. The university in her midwestern city has both a bachelor's program in art history and a graduate program in business, but its tuition is rather expensive.

Initially, she thought she might save some money by taking the first two years of college at her local community college, where she could also have her considerable learnings in art assessed for prior learning credit. She hoped then to transfer to the university to complete her bachelor's degree and go on to work on her master's. After making some phone calls to the registrars of the two schools, however, she learned that the university in her city does not accept assessment credits in transfer, nor will it accept any credits in the student's major that were earned at a community college. If she wants to use her prior learning toward her degree, she will have to register initially at the university and have her learning assessed there. By taking the initiative to do the research before she registered, Joan has saved herself a lot of duplication of effort and frustration.

Independent Learning

Going back to college, even obtaining a college degree, doesn't necessarily mean that you have to attend classes in the traditional way for a certain number of hours per week. Perhaps you live in a rural area, quite far from the nearest school and without access to transportation. Perhaps you have two toddlers and no one with whom to leave them. Or your work may call for a tremendous amount of travel, which makes it unlikely that you could get to class regularly. Or you may be housebound by illness or a handicapping condition. Or you may simply prefer independent to class study. In any case, there are a number of ways in which you can get a college education without taking all your courses and earning all your credit sitting in a traditional classroom.

Seven well-known "independent learning" colleges have joined together to make their programs available to adult learners for whom traditional classroom study is not an option (see Appendix D for a list with addresses and telephone numbers). These colleges have the capacity to work with students from anywhere in the country. Each is committed to finding ways to support the student who rarely, if ever, can attend a class or meet face-to-face with a professor. Each has graduated thousands of adults whose

Participating in an independent program requires the ability to study and learn on your own. You will be setting your own study hours and exercising self-discipline in completing your assignments.

degrees have opened up for them avenues of personal and professional advancement. All of them offer assessment of prior learning, and all of them accommodate part-time study.

Other, more traditional colleges and universities frequently offer a wide range of options, including independent study, study at extension divisions, credit for correspondence or television courses and other comparable ways of learning. Check this out at your local college.

Participating in an independent program requires a strong commitment to learning and the ability to learn on your own. It means that you will have to reschedule your life to find regular time for study and enlist the understanding of other members of your household. It may mean making use of local learning resources, such as libraries, television programs, museums, workplaces, churches, videos and computers. At some schools it may mean working with faculty to design your own learning contracts — that is, deciding what you intend to study, what learning resources you will use, what activities you will carry out, and what criteria will be used to evaluate your progress. In other schools you may be working on courses with preset written, taped or computer materials. You may be communicating with the professor by telephone, fax, modem or mail. You will be setting your own study hours and exercising self-discipline in completing your assignments, keeping in touch with the professor or mentor, and persevering toward completion and success.

Many independent learners miss the opportunity to exchange ideas with their teachers and other students in a face-to-face situation, to discuss, to argue, to get different points of view. Recognizing the importance of such interchange, some of the colleges that offer independent learning options have set up weekend seminars or two-week summer workshops at which independent learners can meet on topics of common interest and learn together.

The colleges that offer independent learning have given thousands of adult students the freedom to work from their own homes, at their own pace, and on their own schedule. On farms, in small towns, in nursing homes, in large cities, even in prisons, people who might otherwise have had to give up their dreams of a college education are participating in independent learning opportunities.

Learning to "Speak College"

An important determinant of your choice of schools is whether what you need is simply a few courses, credit or non-credit, a certificate or a degree. The next thing you want to understand is the meaning of these terms.

Noncredit courses. These are offered by a variety of institutions to fulfill the needs of people for instruction in the arts and sciences, professional fields, self-help (such as time management and holistic healing), personal enrichment (poetry writing, wine tasting, stenciling) and vocational skills. There are no rules about how long these courses should be or who should be permitted to teach them. The non-credit offerings at some institutions, however, are among the most innovative learning opportunities in the country.

Credit courses. These are offered by accredited colleges and universities and typically take about 12 to 15 hours of classroom time per credit (with equal or double that expected in reading and research outside the classroom). A credit course may be part of a degree or certificate program or may simply be taken as a single entity. It may take place over the period of a semester, a month or a single intensive weekend.

Continuing education units (CEUs). CEUs are nontraditional credit carried by some continuing education courses designed to meet the requirements of specific professional organizations in areas such as nursing, law, medicine, social work, accounting, and engineering. Since CEUs are awarded on the basis of attendance rather than of learning acquired, most schools do not equate them with college credit.

Certificate programs. These are designed to cover a specific field, such as management information systems, paralegal studies or auto body repair. They may consist of anywhere from 2 to 12 courses and may be open in some cases to people with no previous college experience. In other cases a college degree or certain relevant courses may be prerequisites. In some situations a certificate can be earned on the way to getting a degree, and the credits earned will apply to that degree. (If you want to keep all options open, you will want to check this out prior to beginning a certificate program.)

Associate's degrees. These include the associate of arts (A.A.), the associate of science (A.S.), the associate of applied science (A.A.S.), the associate of professional studies (A.P.S.) and a number of variations. The associate's is typically a two-year degree requiring about 60 credits.[1] (Part-time study may increase the time to four or six years.) In some, but not all, cases the credits can be transferred to a four-year college.

Bachelor's degrees. These include the bachelor of arts (B.A.), the bachelor of science (B.S.), the bachelor of professional studies (B.P.S.) and numerous variations. The bachelor's degree usually requires about 120 credits (four years of full-time study).

Master's degrees. These include the master of arts (M.A.), the master of science (M.S.), master of library science (M.L.S.), master of social work (M.S.W), etc. They are typically 30- to 36-credit programs (beyond the bachelor's degree) and may require a research project culminating in the writing of a thesis. Some master's programs include a substantial amount of field work.

Doctoral degrees. These include the doctor of philosophy (Ph.D.), the doctor of laws (LL.D. or J.D.), the doctor of medicine (M.D.), the doctor of education (Ed.D.), etc. They usually require about 60 hours of graduate study, and most require completion of a major research study or dissertation.

---

1. In the description of this and other degrees, the average time stated is for full-time study, which generally means taking from 12 to 15 credits per semester. Since most adult students cannot study full time, the length of time needed to complete the degree may be double or more.

Credit versus Non-Credit Study

Don't let all of this discussion of degrees make you think that learning is worthwhile only if you get a piece of paper saying you have earned a few initials. Not everyone wants or needs to study toward a degree. Indeed, there are advantages to nondegree study:

- You can learn what you want or need to learn without having to take specific courses to fulfill degree requirements.

- You can go at your own pace, in credit or noncredit courses.

- You can concentrate less on grades and more on what you are learning for its own sake.

And, of course there are also advantages to degrees or certificates:

- Degrees and certificates are passports to some jobs in real estate, teaching, business management, etc.

- They are necessary for some licensed professions such as engineering, nursing, dentistry and accounting.

- A degree or certificate signifies to the world and yourself that you have acquired a significant amount of learning in a particular field.

- A degree is more easily transferable than a collection of courses if you wish to go on for a higher degree.

- You have something to hang on the wall that people recognize.

Getting the Information You Need

Earlier we compared choosing a school with choosing a new car or washing machine or place to vacation. You have probably come to the conclusion that choosing a school makes the other decisions look easy, and you may be getting nervous about how to get all the information you want.

It's really not that difficult. If you were choosing a place to vacation, you would probably begin by deciding on the high-priority items for you and your family (musts and wants). Let's say you wanted to find a place that was warm, near the water so your children could swim and you could fish, near a golf course, and relatively inexpensive.

You might begin by talking to friends who had recently gone away. Let's say a few of them recommended Florida, but disagreed on whether you should go to the east or west coast or whether you should stay at a beach hotel, a motel on the bay, or a resort near Disneyworld.

You might then read an article in a travel magazine, which would give you more specific information on Florida, and you would probably want to talk to a travel agent to find out about the various resorts available.

Your next step would probably be to look over some brochures that you received from the travel agent or that you had written away for. You would compare locations, facilities, prices and general attractiveness. As in all decisions, you would have to set some priorities: should you pay more to stay in a hotel with a great restaurant, or is it better to have your own kitchen? would you rather be right on the beach, a block away where the rent is lower, or back in the town? Should you pass up a terrific bargain in Miami Beach to be closer to friends who live in Tampa?

Finding out about schools is not as different from this process — or as difficult — as you may think. You have a similar range of resources for information:

■ friends and relatives who have gone back to school;

■ college admissions officers, counselors and professors;

■ the guidance counselor at your local high school;

■ the human resources or training specialist at your place of employment;

■ public information sessions that are given at many colleges; and

- printed materials (college catalogs and brochures [available in libraries and your local high school, but you can also order them by phone directly from the colleges], standard college guides like Barron's or Peterson's [available in libraries], ads and articles in the education section of your newspaper.)

Using College Catalogs

The college catalog is the primary way in which a school communicates with prospective students. It contains a wealth of information about the mission of the institution, its status with state and national accrediting agencies, its range of degrees and programs, its educational philosophy and the degrees and attainments of its faculty. It has detailed information about such practical matters as admissions policies, tuition charges, degrees offered, course and credit requirements, the school calendar, grading, special programs and the like.

The catalog is also a public relations tool, however. It is carefully designed to present the image the school wishes to convey. A careful reading of the catalog, including a close look at the illustrations, will tell you a great deal about the institution that will be valuable to you in making your choice, but you will probably have to discover many things, both positive and negative, for yourself. If you can find answers to the list of questions in Exercise 4-2, you'll have a good general sense of what you can expect from a college and what it will expect from you. An up-close, properly skeptical look at the catalog of the school you plan to attend will answer most of these questions as well as others you may have.

Once you have acquired this general information and have determined that you want your knowledge assessed for college credit, you will also need some information on the institution's views of, and procedures for, the assignment of credit for prior learning. Exercise 4-3 poses some questions on this issue for which you will want answers.

Many of these questions may seem a bit overwhelming, but it is important that you get the answers before you register, not

Exercise 4-2: Important Questions to Ask about Colleges

1. What are the admissions criteria for adults in this school?

2. Is there any special reference to adult or nontraditional students under admissions policies?

3. Are there any prerequisites (courses you should already have completed) for the course/program you are planning to take?

4. What department gives the course/program you want? (If it is a noncredit course, it may be in the continuing education bulletin and not in this catalog.)

5. How long will it take you to complete the program or degree? To figure this out you will have to know:

   ■ the total number of courses in the program/degree;

   ■ the number of courses you may have already completed through an earlier time in college, through evaluated coursework in a military or corporate setting, or through an assessment for learning you have accomplished on your own; and

   ■ how many courses you expect to take per semester or per year

6. Is there a program of prior learning assessment or admission with advanced standing? (See Exercise 4-3 for a list of more specific questions you should ask about prior learning assessment.)

7. Is any mention made of whether degrees can be completed on a part-time basis, or does the school require full-time status?

8. Are adult students or working students mentioned (or pictured) at all? How often?

9. Is it clear from the catalog whether one can complete a degree by taking courses in the late afternoon, evenings or weekends?   →

10. How much time do you have at the beginning of a semester to withdraw from a course without penalty?

11. Does the school have the following services available for adult students?

    ■ child care (late afternoons and evenings)
    ■ career counseling
    ■ academic advising
    ■ financial aid
    ■ basic skills workshops or tutoring

12. Do adult students have to fulfill requirements that are more appropriate to younger students, such as physical education, payment of student activity or health fees?

13. What fees does the school charge in addition to tuition?

14. Are there many pictures in the catalog of older people or minorities?

15. What kind of clothes are the students wearing? Are they dressed up or casual?

16. Do the pictures of classrooms show large lecture sections or smaller, more intimate groups?

after. More than likely, your institution will have a well-staffed prior learning assessment office, an adult learning service office, a testing and assessment office, a continuing education department, or an external degree programs office, with counselors or advisors who can give you the answers you need. Sample tests and preparation booklets for CLEP and other exams should be available. If you are interested in a portfolio assessment option, they may also have samples of other students' portfolios for you to review.

Don't be afraid to ask other questions you may have, no matter how unimportant they may seem. Undertaking the assessment process requires a strong commitment of time, effort, and money. You want to be sure that you have as clear a picture as

Exercise 4-3: What You Need to Find Out about Assessment

1. Does the institution you plan to attend give credit or recognition for learning acquired outside a formal school setting?

2. Does it offer some or all of the following alternatives?

   - Portfolio assessment
   - Credit by examination (CLEP, ACT-PEP, DANTES, SOCAT)
   - Challenge exams
   - Acceptance of ACE recommendations on noncollegiate sponsored instruction (PONSI)
   - Acceptance of ACE recommendations on military education
   - Other

3. Does the institution limit the number of credits you can earn by way of these methods? (At some institutions, separate limits are set on credits earned by each means — credit by examination, correspondence, PONSI, ACE military, or portfolio. At others they are lumped together. Make sure you find out your institution's policy before you begin. You want to be sure that the options offered will work to your advantage.)

4. Can credits earned through assessment apply to any aspect of your degree program or only to a selected portion — to your major, for example, or only to free electives?

5. Will credits awarded for your prior learning, through any of the means offered above, be applied to your degree program immediately or only after particular course requirements have been met?

6. When can you begin the assessment process?

   - before you register at the college?
   - during the first semester?
   - after you have met certain requirements?
   - anytime?   →

7. What printed materials, guidelines, and forms are provided for you to use?

8. If you have selected portfolio-assisted assessment, what personal assistance does the institution provide, such as workshops, advisors, or a course on assessment?

9. Is there a restriction on the length of time in which you must complete your portfolio or other forms of assessment?

10. If you choose to do a portfolio, who will assess it after it is developed?

   ■ college faculty
   ■ assessment office personnel
   ■ experts external to the institution

11. How and by whom are credit recommendations made?

12. Can you appeal a credit recommendation decision if it does not seem fair? If so, how?

13. What are the fees? Is there a blanket charge for assessment, or will you be charged by the credit? If the latter, is it based on the credits requested or the credit granted? And what is the correlation between the fees for assessment and the regular course fees?

14. How much time will the assessment process take? Is the time and cost to your benefit?

15. Does the school's assessment program conform to CAEL's standards for quality assurance (see Appendix A)?

possible of what will be expected of you so that you can put your best effort toward demonstrating that you really do possess the college-level knowledge or competency you claim to have.

Follow-Up Activities

Some kinds of information about how a school "feels" are not readily available, either from people or printed information. To get a real sense of a school, you should probably take yourself on a campus tour, talking to students as well as to school officials, looking over the library, the bookstore, the cafeterias and student "hang outs," perhaps even sitting in on a class or two. Most professors will welcome you if you arrange for such a visit ahead of time. A personal visit is a great way to find out how long it takes to drive to the campus, how crowded the parking lot is, how the dining hall hamburgers taste, and how many students are in your age group. Use the guide in chapter 8, pp. 136–9 to help organize your tour.

Hedging Your Bets

It is important to recognize that what you want today may change, and the decisions you make now about schools, programs and courses may also have to change. At any point in your life the choices you make are conditioned by habits of mind, events and temporary circumstances that can alter. Don't worry too much about possibly making the "wrong" decisions. Many adults have found that returning to school profoundly changes their sense of what they want to accomplish, what they want to study, and how they choose to study it. If, despite serious thinking about it, you're still not sure exactly what you want to do, you're in good company. One of the exciting things about education is that it gets people thinking more explicitly about where they're heading in life and why. Even if you change your mind after six months in school, your early decisions won't be "mistakes" if, as a smart consumer, you have hedged your bets. Some useful strategies for hedging your bets include the following:

■ Start with one or two basic courses that will be useful in a number of different programs. For instance, courses in English are usually required or recommended in any program.

■ Take a basic course in your own specialty to see how you like it and how well you do. If Dorene (see profiles, chapter 2, p. 16) were still uncertain about whether she wanted to work toward a degree in computer science or take a certificate program in management information systems (MIS), she could take a course in computer programming that is a requirement in both.

■ Make certain the courses you take in College A will be easily transferable to Colleges B and C. This enables you to keep open your option to switch schools if your first choice doesn't work out. Introductory courses in basic subjects such as English and mathematics are usually easier to transfer than unusual or specialized courses.

You may wish to return to this chapter more than once as you become involved in the actual process of returning to school, but for now let's turn our attention to the major issue in this book: how to get college credit for learning you have accomplished on your own.

5

Prior Learning Assessment

Getting Credit for What You Know

"And long experience made him sage."
—John Gay

In the previous chapter's discussion on how to choose a college, it was suggested that one of your criteria might be whether or not the school had a program of prior learning assessment. Prior learning assessment (PLA) is a process whereby any learning you have acquired before the assessment and have not had transcripted by a college is evaluated to determine whether it is comparable with what is taught in college and, if so, is recognized by the award of college credit.

In this and the following chapters, we will be looking at all aspects of PLA: why it's useful to adult students, how it works, and what you can do right now to get started on the path to getting credit for what you have learned. But first, if you are like most adults, you're probably wondering whether you have any learning that is "assessable." You may even doubt that you still have the ability to learn. These are legitimate questions that deserve serious thought.

The Adult as an Accomplished Learner

The typical adult's worries about loss of learning abilities are usually groundless. Let us deal first with your doubts about your ability to learn. If you have any teenagers at home, you might compare yourself with them. They may memorize facts or solve mathematical puzzles more quickly than you, but do they have your ability to call upon past knowledge or experience when confronting a problem, to communicate, to use critical reasoning? Do they have the vast number of specific skills you have accumulated that will make learning new ones easier? Do they have as clear a sense of purpose or as strong a commitment to what they are doing?

Adults' experience and maturity give them an advantage over their younger classmates. As students they typically have a better sense of what they want to learn and why, and in order to go back to school they have made sacrifices in time, money and lifestyle that bolster their determination to succeed. As a result, most studies show that adult students do very well in the classroom, typically meeting or exceeding the performance of traditional college-age students.

You as a Learner

You are already an accomplished learner. You've been learning all your life. Just think about the learning you demonstrate just to get through each day. Think about your domestic learning: about how you shop, plan and cook meals, make household repairs, attend to car maintenance, care for children. Or about your work learning: how you function in a factory or office or hospital or store or on the streets of the city. What an enormous number of things you have to know and be able to do to function success-fully. Or think about your non-work-related learning: what do you have to know to prepare the soil for your vegetable garden or carry on a discussion about the drug problem or lead your church choir or refinish your best friend's antique cupboard? To begin to focus on your prior learning, complete Exercise 5-1.

Exercise 5-1: Focusing on a Learning Experience

Think of an important learning experience you've had in the last six months. It might have been on the job, at home, or in your community. You may have learned how to use a computer, set up a tropical fish tank or conduct a mail campaign for the local policemen's benevolent society. Don't worry right now about whether this learning is college level. If you took the time to learn it, it must have been important to you, and it demonstrates your ability as a learner.

Take a few minutes to make some notes about this learning experience:

■ What did you learn?
■ How did you learn it?
■ Where did you learn it?
■ Why did you learn it?

The *what* of learning is important for a prior learning assess-ment program. If you can say I learned to create and use a spread-sheet program on the computer, or I learned to dismantle and repair my VCR, or I learned why taking an accurate census is polit-ically crucial to my party, you will have taken the first step toward recognizing your own learning. This sounds obvious, but the prob-lem many people have in undertaking prior learning assessment is in being specific about naming or defining their own learning. They will say something like, "Well, I know a lot about construc-tion or social work or transportation," but they have difficulty nar-rowing down these terms to define exactly what it is they actually know or can do.

The *how* of learning leads you to recognize the various ways in which adults learn and to begin to understand your own learning style. People learn from watching and listening to experts, from reading, from doing and experimenting, and by comparing past experience with new experience (reflecting).

The *where* of learning should suggest to you the almost endless number of sources of learning in the modern world. We may learn from:

- formal instruction (in school, on the job, in the military, in classes sponsored by churches and community organizations);
- working — on the job experiential learning;
- books, articles and newspapers;
- radio, television and videos;
- observation of other people;
- questioning of friends, relatives, supervisors, experts;
- computer programs; and
- traveling.

Perhaps most profound of all is the *why* of learning. We learn because we need some information or we need to know how to do something. The why of learning is critical, because if we don't have a reason, we won't learn. Some of the reasons people give for learning are to:

- keep up with technological change in the workplace;
- prepare for a new career;
- help get through a difficult life transition, such as divorce, a family death, kids growing up and moving away;
- improve their ability to participate in community affairs;
- become more proficient in a sport or hobby;
- "keep up" with friends or family members;
- get a degree or license or certificate;
- meet new people;
- prepare for retirement;
- get a GED (high school equivalency degree);
- improve their English; and
- achieve the satisfaction of learning something new.

All learning is valuable. If you have taken the time to learn something, the reason was that learning it was going to be useful to you in some way. You should value your learnings and take pride in yourself as a learner, whether or not the things you have learned are similar to what is taught in college. But if you are contemplating returning to college in the near future, or if you have sometimes wished you could go to college without repeating courses in what you already know, you should seriously consider the possibility of assessment of your prior learning for college credit.

The Background of PLA Programs

Assessment of prior learning is not a new idea. Some colleges have for many years had advanced placement programs in which they routinely test incoming freshman for English or foreign language or mathematics skills, placing them in advanced courses in those subjects when they do well. Some professors informally counsel students who are already highly proficient in the materials of an introductory course — computer science, for instance, or basic office procedures — to skip that course and take more advanced classes.

But the practice of assessing of prior learning as a systematic way of finding out what college-level skills and knowledge adult students bring with them and evaluating those skills and knowledge for college credit is less than 50 years old. It can be said to have begun right after World War II, when the American Council on Education (ACE) began offering recommendations for college credit awards for learning in the military services. Formalized testing programs as a means of assessing prior learning made their appearance in the mid-1960s. The assessment movement, however, can be said to have begun in 1974 with an organization called the Council for Adult and Experiential Learning (CAEL). CAEL was interested in the extent and variety of learnings people acquire on their own and was dedicated to researching methods that would enable educational institutions to conduct *valid*, *reliable* assessments of learning acquired outside those institutions.

Since 1974 one of CAEL's major purposes has been to research and promote the formal assessment and recognition of college-level learning of two kinds not commonly recognized by credit or advancement in standing: (1) that acquired before the assessment by the current institution and not previously transcripted and (2) that acquired under the sponsorship of the current institution via practice, internships, apprenticeships, and other hands-on experiences occurring off campus. Today CAEL is active in helping colleges and universities set up programs to examine and evaluate individuals' formal and experiential learnings,[1] and, when they are found equivalent to what is taught in college, grant credit for them. It also has a quality assurance program to monitor and evaluate current assessment programs (see Appendix A).

A number of fine colleges and universities in the United States (and Canada, Great Britain and Australia) have recognized that what adults learn on their own or through their work can be quite similar to what is taught in the classroom. These schools have set up programs to identify, evaluate and award credit for college-level learning no matter where or how it was acquired. (See Appendix J for an annotated list of such institutions in the United States.)

Why PLA Programs Are Important

You may wonder why assessment of prior learning is considered so important. Well, simple fairness is one reason. Suppose Kate, an office worker responsible for keeping the financial records of a small manufacturing company, has taught herself the principles of accounting by working out a functional bookkeeping system, attending company-based training workshops and reading accounting textbooks. Why shouldn't she get the same credit for what she knows as a person who takes Accounting 101 at a local

---

1. Experiential learning is any learning in which the learner is in direct touch with the realities being studied. In other words, it is learning by doing, by hands-on practice. For example, learning management by taking a company-sponsored training class is formal or nonexperiential. Learning management by trial and error as you deal with five persons who work under your supervision is experiential. A combination of nonexperiential learning, which emphasizes theory, and experiential learning, which emphasizes practice, can lead to a richer education than either of these alone.

community college? Or suppose Bill, who has been running a support program for AIDS victims through his church and has learned group counseling techniques from the social workers and minister involved in the program, wants to go back to school to get a degree in social work. Why shouldn't the university to which he has applied evaluate what he has already learned about counseling to see how closely it approximates what is taught in the school's own counseling courses?

Beyond the issue of simple fairness, prior learning assessment programs afford students tremendous savings of time and money. Busy adults who go back to school have to juggle the time spent in class and study along with the demands of jobs and families and community responsibilities. Their time is limited and very valuable to them. If by earning one or two semesters worth of credit through PLA they can shorten the length of time necessary to achieve a degree, the pressures on them will be considerably lighter.

Similarly, most adults returning to school are making a considerable financial sacrifice, paying for tuition, books and supplies, transportation, possibly for baby sitters. If the number of courses they must take is lessened by PLA, the savings can be significant.

Even those adults whose employer is paying for their education through tuition reimbursement or prepaid tuition can benefit financially from PLA. Most tuition plans have a cap or ceiling on the total amount that can be spent on education. If some courses can be recognized through PLA, there may be more funding available for more advanced courses.

PLA is also useful in defining what students *don't* know, which can be very helpful in planning their courses of study. For example, in her job with an international bank, Judy acquired considerable learning in management and finance but had no opportunity to learn much about marketing or customer relations. In going through the PLA process, she not only validated her own strengths in management and finance, she also discovered the limits of her learning and decided to include marketing, consumer psychology and customer relations in her degree program. Jules, who has been working as a designer's assistant for seven years and hopes to earn a degree in industrial design, found out through the assessment process that his experience with computer-aided design (CAD) is too superficial to qualify for college credit. He is planning to take courses in CAD to address this deficiency.

Finally, and perhaps most important, it is gratifying to achieve recognition for learning that you have accomplished on your own. Most people who have gone through the process of prior learning assessment report that as they began to realize the extent and quality of their learning, they gained in confidence and self-esteem.

Today, as more and more adults are going back to the classroom and as the average age of college students in the United States has risen to 32.5 years, hundreds of colleges and universities have recognized the wealth of learning that these adult students bring with them and have responded by offering testing options and/or creating prior learning assessment programs. These programs have enabled thousands of adult learners like yourself to gain recognition and credit for the college-level learning they have accomplished on their own.

If you consult Appendix J for the list of institutions offering PLA, you will probably find one or more in your geographic area. Then, if after finishing this book you think you may qualify for college credit for what you have learned, you will know where to start your search for the school that is right for you.

6

Some Methods Institutions Use to Evaluate Your Prior Learning

"Nothing in education is so astonishing as the amount of ignorance it accumulates in the form of inert facts."
—Henry Brooks Adams

By now you should be convinced that you have indeed acquired considerable learning over your lifetime and that some of that learning may be the equivalent of what you could have learned in college. Let's review some of the methods used to translate learning from life experience into college credits:

1. transfer of transcript credit;
2. articulation agreements among colleges and other institutions;
3. proficiency examinations;

4. credit for the completion of evaluated programs: military, corporate or union;
5. credit for previously evaluated licenses, certificates, apprenticeships; and
6. credit by portfolio-assisted assessment.

In the following pages we will look closely at the first five of these options. In the next chapter we will go into an in-depth explanation of portfolio-assisted assessment, including detailed instructions for developing and assembling the portfolio.

If the number of areas in which you hope to earn credit are limited to learning that derives from a source that can be documented by a transcript or evaluated by an examination, or that is contained in a previously evaluated program, you may not have to produce a portfolio. If your learnings are less "neat," however, that is, if you do not have transcripts, can't locate standardized exams that cover the knowledge you think you have gained, and haven't been involved in programs that have been evaluated, you will probably want to consider the development of a portfolio. If this is the case, you will need to choose a school that offers a portfolio assessment program (see Appendix J).

College Transcripts

A college transcript is an official record of courses taken, grades earned, credit received, and degrees granted. If you attended a college at some time in the past, even if it was 20 or 30 years ago, that college still has all the necessary information about you on file, and some or all of the credit earned may transfer to the institution at which you have chosen to complete your degree. You can obtain a copy of your academic record by writing to the registrar of each school you attended and requesting a transcript. You will need to provide the dates of your attendance and the name or names under which you were registered. (Women who changed their names upon marriage sometimes forget to inform the school of the change, and then wonder why their records seem to be missing.) There is usually a fee of a few dollars for each transcript you request. You can find out the amount of the fee and any other regulations the school may have by calling the registrar's office. Be sure that you sign your request because the registrar will need your authorization in order to release the record.

You can use copies of your old transcripts for your own information or to work with while you are going through the assessment process, but schools will ask for official transcripts when they are asked to accept them as documentation for transfer credit. An official transcript is one which bears the original imprint of the college seal. Usually it must be mailed directly from one college to the other, though some schools will accept an original that is hand delivered by the student as long as the imprint is clear.

Do not be discouraged if your old transcripts contain some mediocre or low grades. Registrars know that most people tend to do much better when they return to school as adults than they did when they were younger. Your grades, as long as they are "C" or better, will probably not have much weight in determining whether credits can be transferred. If you failed courses earlier in your college career, those credits will not transfer, but the presence of several failing grades should not deter you from presenting the transcript.

Some colleges have rules about how "old" the credits are, however. They may have regulations that prevent the acceptance of credits that you earned long ago. This is particularly true in fields in the sciences and technologies, which are constantly changing and in which what you learned 14 years ago may by now have been superseded by new research findings. Some schools also have rules about the total maximum number of credits they will accept. They may restrict credit transfer to subjects other than your major, or they may accept only those courses which are similar to those in their own catalogs. Since schools differ widely in their practices in this regard, questions regarding transferability should become part of your own college interview process.

Don't let these rules discourage you from trying to use as much of your previous credit as possible. If you can make a logical argument for the credit's currency and validity in your degree program (without being rude or combative), you may be able to persuade the officials that it would be fair to make an exception in your case. More than one "rule" has been suspended to accommodate adult students who present a logical case for the validity of using the credit they earned somewhere else.

Articulation Agreements

Some colleges have agreements among themselves to accept one another's transcripted credits, including degrees awarded, without questioning individual courses. This is often the case within geographic regions where there is a close relationship between the community college and the four-year college and where each institution respects the other's academic programs. Other kinds of articulation agreements may exist between a college and a proprietary school with a particularly strong program that the college does not offer, or between a college and a local corporation that offers employee training. In these cases, the student's task in making the case for getting credit for prior learning is made considerably easier. Officials in the assessment office of your school will be able to tell you if any articulation agreement exists that will affect the learnings you plan to present.

Credit by Examination

A number of different examination programs have been created to evaluate learning that has been acquired outside the classroom. One or more of the following kinds of exams may provide a good fit with your learning, in which case taking an exam may prove to be the least complicated way for you to earn credit.[1] (See Appendix E for further information on testing organizations.)

---

1. In addition to the standard examination programs listed below, there are several others sponsored by colleges such as Ohio University, Regents College of the University of the State of New York, and Thomas A. Edison State College in New Jersey. You can find out more about these programs by writing to the sponsoring organization at the addresses provided in Appendix D.

1. *CLEP.* The College Level Examination Program is probably the most widely used method of testing the learning that adults have acquired outside the classroom. It is available at testing centers across the country, including most large public libraries and many community colleges. Where you take the exam is not important; what does matter is the policy of your selected school regarding CLEP exams.

   There are two kinds of CLEP exams: general and subject.

   ■ *General.* Each of the general exams covers material taught in courses that most students take as requirements in the first two years of college. Each is 90 minutes long and, except for the English composition version with essay,[2] each consists entirely of multiple-choice questions to be answered in two separately timed sections. From 3 to 6 semester hours of credit are usually awarded for satisfactory scores on each general examination. General examinations are given in the following areas: English composition, or English composition with essay, humanities, mathematics, social sciences and history, and natural sciences. The general exams are useful if you have broad knowledge in one of these fields equivalent to what you would have learned in the first two years of college.

   You can choose to take all of the general exams or only those with which you feel comfortable. You will not be penalized for doing poorly in the exams, but if your scores meet the college's expectations you can accumulate a substantial amount of college credit. Be sure to check with the institution you have chosen regarding its policy on CLEP general exams.

   ■ *Subject.* Each subject examination covers material taught in an undergraduate course with a similar title at most colleges and universities. A college that accepts CLEP subject exams usually grants the same amount of credit to students earning satisfactory scores as it grants to students passing that course.

---

2. Many schools require the English exam with essay. Check this out before you register for the exam.

2. *ACT-PEP.* The American College Testing Proficiency Examination Program covers over 40 courses, including arts and sciences, business and nursing.

3. *DANTES.* The Defense Activity for Nontraditional Educational Support was originally designed for and available only to military personnel. These tests may now be taken by the civilian population as well. They cover such subject areas as physical science, social science, business, applied technology, foreign languages and mathematics.

4. *SOCAT.* The Student Occupational Competency Achievement Tests are particularly useful for assessing the competency of students with learning in a variety of vocational and technical fields.

5. *AP.* Intended primarily for high school students, advanced placement examinations may be taken by anyone, regardless of age or background. They are in primarily academic subjects such as English, history, chemistry and mathematics.

6. *GRE.* Graduate Record Examinations, ordinarily taken as a prerequisite for admission to graduate school, are occasionally used for assessment of prior learning at the undergraduate level.

7. *Challenge Examinations.* These are exams designed by the school, the department, or the faculty member responsible for the course that corresponds to the area of learning for which you are requesting credit. In other words, if you think that your learning in human anatomy is equivalent to what is being taught in a course in human anatomy, some schools will invite you to take a challenge exam in that subject.

Up to this point, all of the exams discussed have been standardized, that is, they are designed by national organizations to be applicable to a large population and to measure a given level of accomplishment. Challenge exams are not standardized. Unlike standardized national exams, challenge exams may reflect the particular philosophy or interests of the professor who teaches the course and may be based on the textbook for that course. Therefore, a bit of caution is in order. Before making a decision to take a challenge exam, it's wise to review the textbook used in the course and discuss the material to be covered with the teacher.

8. *Oral Examinations.* Colleges will sometimes require that a faculty member review and evaluate your learnings in an interview situation. An oral examination may be highly structured or quite informal. Some faculty will ask you a number of previously prepared questions; others may prefer to simply engage you in a discussion of the subject at hand so they may determine the depth and breadth of your learning. Like challenge exams, oral exams are not standardized and tend to be dependent upon the particular course the instructor is teaching. Discuss this option with your advisor before pursuing a college-based oral exam.

9. *Professional certifying examinations.* These are designed and administered by organizations that want to give their members a means of recognition for their skills. An example is Professional Secretaries International (PSI), a nonprofit association whose aim is to elevate secretarial standards and offer opportunities for professional and personal growth and development. PSI exams cover the following subjects: behavioral science in business, business law, economics and management, accounting, communication applications, and office technology. For further information about the scope of standardized exams and for addresses of sponsoring organizations, see Appendix E.

You've probably heard someone say, "I test poorly," or "I'm not a good test taker." It's true that some people do freeze up when they're asked to take paper and pencil tests; they get nervous and can't do their best. You can learn to be a better test taker, however. If you think testing is the most efficient way for you to earn credit for what you know but are nervous about your test-taking abilities, you can probably get help from your school's academic counselors or basic skills teachers. They can give you some simple techniques that will help you do your best, including such pointers as whether to fill in all answers or to leave blanks when you don't know the right answer. A librarian can also help you find books or articles on the best approach to test taking. Finally, if you plan to take the CLEP or ACT-PEP tests, your bookstore will have books with sample copies of these tests on which you can practice.

Credit for the Completion of Evaluated Programs

Much of the formal adult education and training in the United States takes place in courses sponsored by the military, by corporations and unions, and by such government agencies as the Department of Agriculture. Some of these courses are taught by experts in the field, cover the material in depth, and are highly demanding. If you have taken such a course, your learning may be appropriate for college credit and should be assessed.

There may be a shortcut, however. There are national organizations that evaluate such courses and make credit recommendations. If the course or courses you took have already been evaluated, colleges which accept such recommendations will ask you for evidence or documentation that you actually took the course. If the documentation provided is satisfactory, you will not have to take a test or oral examination. Following are the main sources of information on evaluated programs:

- *Guide for the Program on Non-Collegiate Sponsored Instruction* (PONSI). Sponsored by the American Council on Education (ACE), the recommendations of which are widely accepted, PONSI evaluations have been done on several hundred corporate training programs as well as a number of union and government programs. You can find out whether a program you took has been evaluated by looking it up in the PONSI guide in your local library or in the library of the school you are planning to attend.

- *A Guide to the Evaluation of Educational Experiences in the Armed Services*, American Council on Education. Military personnel frequently complete the equivalent of college courses while in the service. These include formal service school courses, correspondence courses with proctored end-of-the-course examinations, Department of Defense (DOD) courses, Army military occupation specialties, and Navy general rates and ratings.

A record of these should appear on your discharge papers. If you were in the service and are uncertain about the status of courses you took, look them up in the ACE Guide or ask the registrar at the school of your choice to review your records of military education. You will need your military discharge papers, DD214, as documentation.

You may also have taken a television, radio or newspaper course or a correspondence course that was sponsored by a college and therefore has already been evaluated. It may require some investigating on your part, but it's well worth your time and effort to learn as much as you can about each of these potentially credit-bearing opportunities.

Credit for Professional Licenses or Certificates

If you are a licensed practical nurse, real estate broker, detective, pilot, vocational education teacher or a member of some other profession that has testing requirements, or if you have completed an apprenticeship in the automotive or building or other trades, you may find that getting credit for what you have learned is made easier. Some colleges have recognized specific professional credentials and licenses as representing a fixed amount of college-level learning, and in those colleges mechanisms for granting credit are already in place. In such a case, it is a fairly simple matter to "prove" that you have the credential. The assessment counselor or head of the assessment program at the school of your choice should be able to tell you if your particular license or credential has already been evaluated.

Sample Applications of Assessment Methods

All of these methods of assessment may be used alone or as part of your portfolio-assisted assessment. Let's look at how some of the people in the profiles in chapter 2 have approached making choices among assessment modes.

Scott's learnings, though extensive and varied, do not fit easily into standard test categories. Therefore, he has chosen to assemble a portfolio that will describe and document his learning.

Scott's learnings, though extensive and varied, do not fit easily into standard test categories. Nor were any of them acquired through formal company-sponsored training that might have been evaluated. Therefore, he has chosen to assemble a portfolio that will describe and document his learning.

Joan's background includes a mixture of conventional and highly individualized learning. She plans to take two of the general CLEP exams, English and humanities, based on her ability to write well and on her general knowledge of literature, music and art. In addition, she will take the DANTES exam on counseling, which she thinks may reflect what she learned in her work with Alcoholics Anonymous. She will incorporate the outcomes of these exams, along with descriptions and documentation for her other learnings in art, film and community organization, into a portfolio.

Dorene has had a difficult time deciding among the many assessment options open to her. Her present plans are to take the CLEP subject exam in college Spanish, levels 1 and 2. She is also going to find out whether the company-sponsored courses she took in word processing and database management have been evaluated. If not, she will also take the CLEP exam in information systems and computer applications (one test).

In order to evaluate her considerable office skills, she is investigating the tests given by Professional Secretaries International (PSI) through its Institute for Certifying Secretaries. She feels that she may be able to pass the tests on behavioral science in business, office technology, and communication applications.

Dorene's union-sponsored courses in labor relations and labor history are listed in the PONSI guide as recommended for credit, so she expects to receive credit for them.

Because of the variety of her learnings and her need to weave this all together in a coherent package, Dorene plans to develop a portfolio that will incorporate the results of tests and evaluated programs along with descriptions and documentation of her learnings in computer applications and Puerto Rican politics and literature.

Max has already taken and has passed the five general CLEP tests. Now he is looking into whether the company-sponsored courses he took while working on the assembly line of a car manufacturing company have been evaluated in the PONSI guide. He will also consult the ACE Guide to the Evaluation of Educational Experiences in the Armed Services to see whether any of the courses he took before being sent to Vietnam are listed.

Max feels that his counseling work with the black youth group and his knowledge of music theory and performance should be evaluated by representatives of the departments of social work and music at his college of choice, so he plans to incorporate all of his learnings into a portfolio.

It was difficult for her college counselor to convince Anna that she had learned anything at all on her own that was worth college credit. Initially she just kept saying that she was a housewife and didn't know anything that was worth college credit. But now that she has accepted the idea that she is an accomplished learner, a gifted cook, and an able administrator, she is busy making lists of her learnings and is beginning to assemble documentation for them.

Anna is terrified of tests, so even though she has been told she could probably pass a test on child psychology, and possibly in English and social studies as well, she plans to present all of her learnings through portfolio-assisted assessment.

C h a p t e r

7

Portfolio-Assisted Assessment

*"Nothing ever becomes real
till it is experienced."*
—John Keats

In the previous chapter we talked about some of the ways in which adults can earn college credit for their prior learning through presenting documents (transcripts and/or apprenticeship records, records of military or corporate training courses evaluated by the American Council for Education) or through taking tests (CLEP, ACT-PEP, DANTES, challenge exams, etc.). Not all kinds of valid learning, however, are recorded on transcripts or can be measured by standardized tests. Learning acquired outside the classroom may have been accumulated over an extended period of time or in a number of different situations, and there may be no easily obtainable "proof" that you have acquired it. Moreover, since extracollegiate learning frequently does not fall into neatly labeled categories, there may be no standardized exams that address exactly what you have learned.

Many schools, seeking a way to validate the knowledge and competencies gained by adults outside the classroom, have adopted portfolio-assisted assessment as a reliable and flexible way of enabling people to define and explain the learning they have gained from experience and to give evidence of the validity of that learning.

What is a Portfolio?

A portfolio is a formal written communication, presented by the student to the college, requesting credit or recognition for extra-collegiate learning. The portfolio must make its case by identifying learning clearly and succinctly, and it must provide sufficient supporting information and documentation so that faculty can use it, alone or in combination with other evidence, as the basis for their evaluation.

In addition to the portfolio's immediate use for gaining credit for learning through assessment, it can also be an invaluable document as the student applies for jobs or further educational opportunities. Moreover, most people find that their portfolio becomes a very precious personal record of their accomplishments as learning adults.

Remember, colleges award credit not for the experiences you have had but for the learning. If you were named athlete of the year or won a promotion to sales manager over 10 other applicants or successfully completed an Outward Bound course, that is undoubtedly a source of considerable satisfaction to you, but it represents an experience. What you must demonstrate to a college assessor is what skills or learning preceded or resulted from that experience. The portfolio gives you the opportunity to do just that.[1]

1. Although putting together a portfolio can be a complicated and even difficult task, there is help available to you beyond the pages of this book. Schools that have portfolio-assisted assessment also have counselors familiar with the system whose job it is to assist you. Many schools also have portfolio workshops, credit or noncredit, in which you can learn more about the process and get help in putting together a document that will reflect your own skills and competencies.

Parts of the Portfolio

Although the specific requirements for a portfolio may vary somewhat from school to school, they almost all have certain standard elements in common. These are:

1. *Identification and definition* of specific prior learning for which college credit is being requested, including competency statements in each area of knowledge;

2. *An essay or narrative* explaining how this prior learning relates to the student's projected degree program, from what experiences it was gained and how it fits into his or her overall education and career plans;

3. *Documentation*, or evidence, that the student has actually acquired the learning he or she is claiming; and

4. *A credit request* listing exactly how much credit the student is asking for in each subject or area.

Identification & Definition of Prior Experiential Learning

This first section of your portfolio should begin with an annotated list of those potentially college-level learnings that you have acquired through classroom experiences beyond high school, through formal training or experience at work, through the armed services, or through hobbies, reading or travel, or in any of the other ways in which people learn. You might reread the section "You as a Learner," chapter 5, to refresh your memory on some of the learnings you have already identified.

One way to begin is to prepare an informal learning resume — a chronological list of your jobs and other learning experiences, including a description of exactly what you had to know or be able to do to function in those experiences. The list will probably start after high school and go up to the present. Take time to think about your past, reviewing what you have learned and where you have learned it. (See "Prior Learning Checklist," Appendix F.)

Your portfolio should begin with an annotated list of those potentially college-level learnings that you have acquired through classroom experiences beyond high school, through formal training or experiences at work, through the armed services, or through hobbies, reading, or travel, or in any of the other ways in which people learn.

You might start with your standard work resume, if you have one, or with a list of the jobs you have held. What were your job titles? What were your responsibilities in each job? What did you do on the job, and what did you have to know to do those things? If you were a line supervisor in a small parts factory, how many people reported to you or for how many people were you responsible? What exactly were those responsibilities? What did you have to know about the manufacturing process to do your job? About the product? About union rules? About getting along with people? Were you responsible for maintenance of the machinery? What else were you supposed to do?

Then go on to non-job experiences that have involved learning: hobbies; sports; family care; creative activities such as painting or playing an instrument; military service; community activities such as volunteer work in a hospital or nursing home, counseling, delivering meals on wheels; and intellectual pursuits such as reading history or philosophy, writing articles or stories, doing biology experiments on your own. What did you learn? How did you learn it? What were you able to do?

Sometimes just "naming" your learnings can be difficult. Learning gained through experience isn't always "neat," and people's skills and competencies aren't always gained in the same logical sequence that college professors use to structure their courses. In each case, the challenge is to go beyond what you actually did in any specific activity or area to what you had to have learned in order to do it. That is, if you say you can manage a high school football team, what does that mean? What skills or knowledge are called for in managing a high school football team? Here are some suggestions, which you may or may not think are part of managing:

- Knowledge of the rules of football;
- Understanding of each team player's capabilities, weaknesses and strengths, psychological makeup;
- Ability to schedule a season that pits your team against comparable teams;
- Ability to schedule tryouts, practice sessions, periods of rest;
- First aid ability;

- Understanding of group psychology and how to make a group function effectively as a team;

- Ability to design strategies and new plays;

- Ability to work well with academic teachers, advisers and administrators; and

- Ability to handle or delegate issues relating to finance, personnel, public relations, ticket sales.

This list could go on and on. Managing a high school football team turns out to be an extraordinarily complicated job involving a number of different kinds of learning. Moreover, since most schools don't teach a course called "Managing Football Teams," these learnings would probably end up by being listed under more conventional course-related headings such as physical education, psychology and management.

Let's look at the people in our profiles to see what kinds of learning lists they might produce.[2]

Scott A.

Scott originally said that he had "no real learning to speak of," certainly nothing that a college might be interested in. After a conversation with the assessment counselor at the local community college, however, he began to look with more respect at what he has learned.

Scott's experience with the lumber industry has been a source of considerable learning about forestry: he knows how to operate and maintain the heavy machinery involved in cutting and transporting lumber; from the time he spent in the seed orchards he knows how to plant new trees (the best species, desirable soil and geographical conditions, maintenance) and understands the concept of reforestation; he has learned something about the economy of timbering and, through 18 months spent at the company's paper mill, has an understanding of the process of turning wood

---

2. Scott's list, as well as the others that follow, assumes that he has already begun to talk to a college assessment counselor and is therefore trying to express his learnings in terms roughly equivalent to college courses.

into paper. Both from workshops sponsored by the company and from his experience in the field, Scott has also learned a great deal about logging safety.

Scott is also a savvy bass fisherman who has learned where to look for fish in different river and weather conditions, how to choose bait, place his cast, and haul in the fish without breaking his line. But he didn't think this was worth mentioning until his assessment counselor told him that the physical education department of the local community college offers a beginner's course in fishing for which he might be eligible for credit.

Through Scott's Bible study group, he has gained an extensive knowledge of both the Old and New Testaments and has begun to understand that they have a historical, religious and literary significance that goes beyond the literal text. He has led group Bible discussions for about three years and feels that he has learned some important things not only about his own religion but beyond his church's interpretation of the texts. He has also studied the origin of religious texts as well as how to prepare for leading group discussions. He was encouraged to list these learnings for possible evaluation by a member of the school's religion and philosophy department.

Scott's hobby is making furniture. His tables and desks are much in demand in his local community, and last year he won first prize in a local crafts show for a birch end-table that he had both designed and made. The school he is planning to attend offers a few crafts courses in making pottery and jewelry, but none in furniture making. Scott has been encouraged by his assessment counselor to ask the head of the crafts program if his skills in furniture-making might be eligible for credit.

A list of Scott's learning experiences is shown in Exhibit 7-1.

Joan B.

Joan's prior learning list is very different from Scott's, but like him she found that it included a lot of learning she had always taken for granted without realizing that it might be similar to what colleges were teaching.

Exhibit 7-1: Scott's Learning Experiences

Source, Date	*Nature of Experience*	*Description of Scott's Learnings*
Perkins' Grocery, part-time 1959–1961	Stocking boy	■ Knows how to stock shelves, putting older items in front, straightening them for neatness, marking prices accurately, checking invoices against merchandise
Eureka Paper Co., 1962–present	Logging	■ Knows how to drive, use, maintain heavy machinery (skidders, tractors, logging trucks, de-limbers, chain saws)
		■ Reforestation: knows desirable soil and terrain conditions; planting, thinning, harvesting techniques; principles of forest ecology
		■ Teamwork: knows how to get along with other members of work team, problem solve, cooperate with management
		■ Logging safety: knows OSHA regulations
1971–1973	Working in Eureka's paper mill	■ Knows production line techniques, chemistry of paper making, technology of paper making

Source, Date	Nature of Experience	Description of Scott's Learnings
Union Methodist Church, 1978–present	Participating in and leading Bible discussion group	■ Knows Old and New Testaments; historical, religious, literary significance of Bible
Hobby, 1955–present	Fishing	■ Has skill in casting, fly tying, catching/landing the fish ■ Knows fish habitat, best weather and water conditions ■ Has skill in boat handling, knows local waters
Hobby, 1970–present	Designing and making furniture	■ Has skill in basic carpentry and woodworking ■ Knows properties of different varieties of wood ■ Knows finishing and refinishing techniques ■ Knows some principles of furniture design ■ Knowledgeable about 19th-century American furniture, its construction and design

Exhibit 7-2: Joan's Learning Experiences

Source, Date	*Nature of Experience*	*Description of Joan's Learnings*
Morse College	Attended college for one semester (12 credits)	■ Studied English composition, European history, music appreciation and organic chemistry
Art galleries, art journals, 1964–present	Reading and observing	■ Knows work of major modern painters and sculptors; can discuss characteristics major contemporary schools of art; is familiar with terminology, media
Dance recitals, books and films on modern dance, 1968–present	Reading and observing	■ Knows and understands techniques of modern dance; characteristics of modern dancers, directors and companies
Fine Arts Museum 1987–1988	Attended training program, three days per week for six months	■ Learned about major periods of western art, major artists
		■ Did research on Egyptian art — learned about period, styles, media, relationship of art to culture, research techniques, how to organize and write a research paper

Source, Date	Nature of Experience	Description of Joan's Learnings
		■ Learned to organize and present a lecture on art to a group of people
		■ Learned about the scope of a museum's collection, and how decisions are made about buying and de-accessioning
Making a film with friends, 1985–1986	Collaborated on script writing, directing, financing	■ Learned how to write film script, principles of film directing, production techniques, marketing and public relations
Alcoholics Anonymous, 1984–1988	Participated as wife of alcoholic, reading about addiction	■ Learned about physical and psychological aspects of substance abuse, how group dynamics work, spouse's role in helping an addict
Al Anon, 1988–1989	Led Al Anon group	■ Learned group dynamics, the responsibilities of a leader, how to deal with participants' stress, how to control own emotions

To become a docent at the local art museum, Joan had gone through a six-month training period with the director of the museum and his staff. During that time she not only became familiar with the major periods of art covered in the museum's collection but had learned how to do oral presentations for groups of tourists and students.

After this first phase of training was complete, each docent was asked to choose one period of art in which to specialize, doing extensive reading and viewing of slides and other collections in that period and writing a research paper. Joan chose to specialize in Egyptian art. As part of her research, she read books and articles about ancient Egyptian history, culture and architecture. She learned enough hieroglyphics to be able to read some of the inscriptions on the tombs and monuments, and she wrote a paper on the monuments of the Upper Nile. When the museum director realized how knowledgeable Joan had become in Egyptology, he asked her to give a talk in the evening public lecture series and invited her to consult with the museum librarian about increasing their holdings in visual and print materials on Egypt.

Joan's experience in working with a friend on a film about artists in the city was also a rich source of learnings about how to write a script, direct the actors and camera people and other technicians, and produce a low budget film that was good enough to be shown in a number of high schools throughout the city.

In her efforts to save her marriage by helping her alcoholic husband conquer his addiction, Joan had become familiar with the physical and emotional dimensions of substance abuse, and through reading and involvement with Alcoholics Anonymous she had learned how group process works to help the addict. For the past few years, Joan has been leading an Al Anon group, for which she prepares by extensive reading in the theory of group interaction and attendance at leadership seminars sponsored by the church.

Joan's first attempt at listing her learnings is shown in Exhibit 7-2.

Dorene G.

When her college assessment counselor first asked Dorene to list those learnings acquired on the job or through other experience, she resisted, saying that she had learned her office skills in high school and didn't know anything in which a college would be interested. When the counselor encouraged her to talk about what she did, however, Dorene soon realized that her extensive competence in a number of business functions went far beyond her own high school learning and beyond that of anyone else in her office. She had become proficient in word processing, knew how to use spreadsheets and had taught herself desktop publishing. She was not only responsible for teaching word processing to new clerical staff but was in charge of designing systems to manage the flow of computer information and was responsible for making decisions about new hardware and software purchases for the office.

Dorene's union activities turned out to be a rich source of learning. Based on the union courses she took, as well as on her actual experience of participating as a union representative in the last two rounds of bargaining with her company, she included contract negotiation in her learning list. She also completed a union-sponsored course in the history of labor relations in the United States, which she thinks covers the same material as the local college's course in that subject.

Neither Dorene nor her counselor are yet ready to predict that her learnings in Puerto Rican history, politics, language and literature will be considered college level or will be equivalent to any college department's offerings. She has included knowledge of the Puerto Rican statehood movement and of Latin American literature in her list of learnings, and she is continuing to study from Spanish language tapes and to read further in the literature of her grandparents' native country.

Max W.

Max's work in the automobile industry has given him a rich background in basic automotive maintenance, engine diagnosis and tune-up, automotive engines and electrical systems, and automotive welding techniques that will probably give him a head start toward an associate's degree in automotive technology.

However, Max has also gained other knowledge and competencies that will enable him to gain credit in nonautomotive areas so as to broaden his degree program. During Max's many years of volunteer work with a black community youth group, he attended a number of church seminars designed to help youth group leaders function more effectively. These seminars, plus his actual experience with the young people and considerable backup reading, may very possibly have given him college-level learning in leadership skills, group process and adolescent psychology.

Max is also an accomplished trumpet player and feels he has the equivalent of at least two college music performance courses. He has put this down on his learnings list, but as the community college he plans to attend teaches music appreciation but not performance, it is not yet clear whether it will agree to evaluate his ability to play an instrument. He has, however, found a course on jazz theory in the college catalog that covers approximately what he knows, and he thinks his knowledge of classical music and theory may be equivalent to what is taught in an introductory music appreciation course.

When Max first talked to the college assessment counselor, he did not even mention the job with which he partially supported himself for the first five years after high school. He had sold tickets and run the projector at a local movie house that specialized in old and foreign films. This job did not at first seem to involve significant learnings beyond using his elementary school arithmetic to make change plus the modest amount of mechanical ability needed to load the projector and perform routine jobs loading and running the projector and doing basic maintenance. The movie house owner had taught him these in a few hours, and Max was pretty sure that they were not college level. But when the counselor asked him why he had stayed for so long in a low paying job, Max enthusiastically explained that he had become fascinated by the movies he ran and had begun reading about film making and film history. In his spare time he went to the local community college's film library, where he was able to view important early films and to follow the progress of certain directors whose techniques fascinated him. Since that time, Max's interest in film has continued, and he spends a lot of his leisure time going to the movies and reading film journals. In fact, when Max looked at the course descriptions in the community college's communications department, he realized that his knowledge of film history was easily equivalent to what he could have learned in the classroom. Exhibit 7-3 lists Max's learning experiences.

Anna P.

Anna had a difficult time assembling her list of learnings. A modest woman, she found it hard to believe that the things she knew and could do, which she took very much for granted, could be worth college credit. An understanding counselor spent considerable time with Anna teasing out descriptions of her learnings and equating them to college level learning. The counselor also helped Anna to see that there is value attached to learning derived from work, regardless of whether that work was paid or done on a volunteer basis. Because Anna is a thoughtful person who deliberates, reads, attends workshops and seminars, and consults other people before she acts, it turned out that she could demonstrate in-depth learnings in a variety of areas. She understands theories of child development as well as the practice of taking care of her own children and the children of others. She had prepared thoroughly for her work with the local cancer society through reading, observation, and discussion with the leaders of other organizations. And in her leadership role there, she had made herself thoroughly familiar with the financial aspects of the organization, had handled the corps of volunteers with skill and diplomacy, and had managed a shrewd public relations campaign that made each year's fund drive more successful than the last. Anna was not only a superb cook, but her culinary skills were

Exhibit 7-3: Max's Learning Experiences

Source, Date	Nature of Experience	Description of Max's Learnings
Globe Movie Theatre, part-time 1974–1978	Working as assistant projectionist	■ Knows operation, maintenance of film projectors ■ Knows American and European films — technique and styles of major directors, understanding of evolution of American film artistry in 20th century
U.S. Coast Guard, 1979–1982	Serving as Seaman 1st Class taking service courses, plus experience	■ Knows basic seamanship, meteorology, electronics
Major Auto Manufacturer, 1983–present	Apprenticing, working	■ Knows automotive maintenance, electric systems, welding and painting, parts warehousing (knowledge of inventory procedures, worker supervision, time management)
Hobby, 1973–present	Taking trumpet lessons; playing trumpet in school orchestra, neighborhood rock band; listening to jazz and classical records; reading *Stereo Review*	■ Plays trumpet at semi-professional level ■ Knows classical and jazz music, musical structures, periods ■ Recognizes major composers and their works

Source, Date	Nature of Experience	Description of Max's Learnings
Volunteer Work with Community Youth Group, 1987–present	Working with troubled teenagers, attending church-sponsored workshops on counseling	■ Has ability to command attention and respect of teenage boys; understands teenage problems with sex, drugs, schools, family; can help troubled kids; works successfully with individual kids and with groups

based on both practice and a knowledge of the basic principles of nutrition and the chemistry of cooking.

College-Level Learning

As you can see, the learning experiences of our five profiled friends cover a wide range of territory. Some occurred in college courses and will be recorded on a transcript (Joan). Some were the result of time in the armed services (Max), formal company or union-sponsored training (Max, Dorene, and Scott), informal on-the-job experience (Scott, Max, and Dorene), volunteer work (Anna and Max), or non-job-related hobbies and interests (all five).

Some jobs, like Max's as projectionist, may offer learning experiences that aren't immediately apparent. So take your time going over your own past history to discover learning experiences. You don't have to finish your list all at once. Give yourself a chance to think about what you have done in your lifetime and what you have learned. The forms in Appendices F and G may be helpful in organizing your list.

Don't ignore those learnings that at first seem to have little to do with what is taught in college. Remember, colleges have physical education departments that may have courses in such sports as tennis, soccer, and swimming. They have sociology or social work departments that may have courses in drug or alcohol counseling or group therapy. They have psychology and education departments that almost certainly teach early childhood development or the psychology of teenagers.

Keep in mind, however, that not all of what Max, Joan, Scott, Dorene and Anna have learned (or what you have learned) is necessarily appropriate for inclusion in a final portfolio. Scott's early experience in a grocery store taught him a lot about responsibility and gave him some fundamental understanding of product stocking and display, but it did not result in any college level learnings. Before proceeding, remember that you must describe your learning in such a way that it meets the following criteria.

College-level learning must:

- be measurable;

- be at a level of achievement defined by the faculty as college equivalent or consistent with the learning of other students engaged in college studies;

- be applicable outside the specific job or context in which it was learned;

- have a knowledge base;

- be reasonably current;

- imply a conceptual or theoretical as well as a practical understanding;

- show some relationship to your degree goals and/or lifelong learning goals; and

- not repeat learning for which credit has already been awarded.

The school you are planning to attend can help you determine the "fit" between your learning and these criteria.

After you have made your initial list of learnings and given yourself a few days or weeks to think about them (and perhaps to add more), you are ready to put together your first version of the formal list of learning components that will actually go into your portfolio. While schools may have different formats for this, the form used by Scott, Max and Joan will be sufficient to get you started assembling your critical information in a way that is clear and easily understandable. Eventually you will need to go back to your list, decide which learning components are potentially college level, and find ways to describe them in greater detail so that they will clearly satisfy the eligibility requirements for college credit listed above).

For example, with the help of her assessment counselor, Joan realized that in her work as a docent she had become quite competent as a public speaker and that her learnings, if fully described, probably covered much of what is taught in Speech 101.

Joan's final description of her learnings in speech looked like this:

> *I can overcome nervousness when talking to groups by making certain that I know the material thoroughly; making eye contact with my audience; checking out my audio-visual equipment ahead of time so that I'm not embarrassed by a nonfunctioning projector or burnt out bulb.*
>
> *To make a presentation sound natural, I prepare thoroughly but speak from an outline, not a written out or memorized speech; I relate information from my own experience; I use natural gestures and employ humor; when asked questions, I invite audience comment.*
>
> *To make certain that the information I provide about the paintings and sculpture comes across accurately and holds the audience's attention, I start with ideas or facts that are particularly interesting; I relate each period, artist or object to something people are likely to already know about; I make clear connections among the various periods, artists and objects; When I want to emphasize a point, I repeat it using different words I make certain that my audience can hear me without straining; I have listened to myself speak on video and have learned how to modulate my voice; I make smooth transitions from one topic to another; I stop frequently to encourage audience comment and to respond to it; I try to frame questions that will provoke discussion and that go beyond a simple yes or no answer. I welcome criticism and accept it gracefully.*

The Essay or Narrative

Most assessment programs require a general essay or narrative in which you tell something about yourself, your experiences, your goals and aspirations, and your reasons for seeking credit for your prior learning. This essay should also show how your present learnings are linked to what you plan to do in college and, in some cases, should include mention of what you haven't yet learned — the gaps in your knowledge and skills that you want to fill in through further education.

Some schools may ask you to do a series of shorter essays supporting each competence area. That is, if you were requesting credit in business management, electronics and Civil War history, you would do a brief essay explaining your learnings in each of these areas — how you acquired them, what is the depth and breadth of your knowledge or skills, how they relate to college-level learning (see above, p. 101), and how they fit in with your general degree program.[3]

Although the essay or narrative is frequently not linked as strongly to the actual credit recommendations as is your documentation, it is a very important component because it communicates *who* you are. College students who attend classes usually have an entire 15-week semester to convey to their professors who they are. Through classroom participation, promptness in completing assignments, and performance in research projects and exams, professors get a pretty good idea of their students' motivation, breadth and quality of knowledge, and the level of their communication skills. In most assessment of prior learning programs, you are expected to accomplish all of this through your portfolio and perhaps an evaluation interview with a faculty member in each of your learning areas.

Clearly, the essay is a major opportunity to introduce yourself to the people who will be making final judgments about the validity of your credit requests. A good essay can convey information about your motivation, competence, and communication skills. It will also help you put your knowledge and experience in perspective.

Although your own institution, if it requires an essay, will probably provide you with its own outline, here are a few suggestions for developing this part of your portfolio.

1. *Begin in a straightforward manner,* that is, state your goals and relate them to your reasons for seeking credit for your prior learning.

3. Descriptions of your learning components will be the heart of your portfolio. Depending on your college's preferred outline, they will appear either in the narrative essay of (preferably) in conjunction with your credit requests and support documentation.

2. *Tell enough about your life so that the assessor gets a sense of who you are and where you are going.* A brief autobiography is a way of conveying your background, your interests, and your personality. While it is not usually appropriate to write about the intimate details of your growing up, your marriage, or your various illnesses, sometimes these things bear directly on your motivation for learning or going back to school. If so, include them but keep your descriptions short and to the point. Don't turn the autobiography into a confessional orgy! Remember, it will become a public document and will be read by strangers.

3. *Use a tone that is self-confident and assertive.* You want to communicate your strengths and accomplishments and also give the reader a sense of your motivation. Are you completing something started long ago or seeking a job promotion? Whatever the motivating factor is for you to want to earn credits through the assessment process, let it come across in your tone.

   The most impressive essays or narratives convey not only the factors that have contributed to a person's experience or growth but also some sense of excitement about continuing that experience or growth in a new direction, with greater understanding and motivation.

4. *Organize your essay or narrative in a clear, logical and comfortable way.* You may wish to do this chronologically (by time sequence) or by subject matter; whatever feels right to you will probably produce the best results.

5. *Be sure that you are addressing what is important to the institution.* Some institutions seek complete autobiographies; others consider only the learning experiences directly related to your request for credit. Read carefully the description of the essay that your institution uses in its portfolio assessment literature, and make certain that you include everything it considers relevant.

6. *Develop a conclusion.* Make sure that the end of your essay or narrative sums up why you are seeking to earn credits through portfolio-assisted assessment and what this will mean to your future. Although there is no formula for a perfect conclusion, you will want to make certain yours is consistent with the rest of your text and is positive in tone.

7. *Edit, edit, edit.* Get an early start on the essay so that you can put the first draft away for a while and then, when you can approach it afresh and see your mistakes, rewrite it. Not even Hemingway tried to publish his first drafts.

It may also help to have a friend who writes well or a former teacher look over the essay to make certain there are no obvious grammatical or spelling errors and, even more important, that it says what you mean it to say.

Don't be intimidated at the prospect of writing an essay. Although many adults approach it as a difficult task, it can be one of the most rewarding experiences of the assessment process. The essay offers you a unique opportunity to reflect on your past, gain a new understanding of yourself and all you've accomplished in your life, and anticipate with confidence your future plans and objectives.

Documenting Your Skills and Knowledge

The purpose of the documentation section of your portfolio is to provide evidence of your having acquired the learnings described in your portfolio. Just as students in a classroom must provide evidence of their learning in the form of book reports, oral presentations, research papers or examination results, so too, you will be expected to demonstrate that you really do possess the knowledge or skills you claim to have.

Documentation may take many forms: a computer program you've designed; an official transcript of a company training course you've taken; a tape of a piano recital you gave; a letter from a former employer outlining your job responsibilities and describing your performance. In this section, we will look at different kinds of documentation you may be able to use and discuss how best to obtain that documentation.

Documentation Resources

No doubt when you were listing your work and learning activities, you recalled specific people, projects, or reports that were critical to your success. These could serve as your documentation resources. In fact, it would be useful to go back to that form and add a column on the right in which you can list possible documentation for each learning component.

Documentation resources usually fall into two categories: direct and indirect. Direct documentation refers to products you have created, performances you have given, reports you have written, marketing plans you have produced, etc. In most cases, direct documentation serves as the strongest evidence that you really do know what you say you know or have the skills you say you have. You must be prepared to prove, however, that the evidence or product was created by you.

Examples of direct documentation include:

- management reports you have compiled and written, in whole or in part;
- photographs you have taken;
- articles, plays, poems or stories you have written;
- audio or audiovisual tapes of speeches, talks, training or performances you have given;
- blueprints of electronic circuits or buildings you have designed;
- musical scores you have arranged;
- computer programs you have designed;
- manuals or brochures you have written or designed;
- patents you have obtained;
- curriculum plans you have prepared; or
- paintings, sculptures or drawings you have created.

In all of these forms of direct documentation, there must be some form of validation that the photograph or tape or computer program is really yours or a clear indication of the part you actually played in the preparation of the whole. Original signatures, printed acknowledgments or accompanying letters of confirmation, etc. may provide that validation.

Indirect documentation is usually information *about* you and your accomplishments. It can take the form of:

- letters written on your behalf by employers, co-workers, business partners, business consultants, teachers, church, community or government leaders, or professional association members;

- commendations you may have received (awards, medals, official recommendations);

- official personnel evaluations by your supervisor;

- transcripts showing test results or college courses passed or documenting completion of training programs;

- program notes from performances you have given or exhibits in which you have shown your work; or

- magazine or newspaper articles about you and your accomplishments;

Weak sources of documentation, which should be avoided, include:

- letters from family members, your own students or clients, your own employees, or friends who might serve as "personal references" in other contexts;

- travel brochures of places you have visited;

- newspaper clippings about events in which you say you participated but which do not mention you; or job evaluations that are not specific about what you actually did or what skills you exhibited; an evaluation that merely states you were a good employee, or even a superb employee, is poor documentation for your skills and learnings.

Documentation Steps

1. *Identify what you know.*

You can only begin to think about documenting your knowledge after it's been identified. Before requesting or assembling your documentation, be sure you know exactly what learning it is you're trying to verify (refer to the list of learnings that you compiled earlier in this chapter). Feel free to consult with the college you are planning to attend for assistance with this process.

2. *List your documentation resources.*

   A. For direct documentation, inventory the pieces you plan to use. Do you know where they are? Where did you put your copy of your last personnel evaluation? Is your best painting on the wall in your local library or in your studio? Is a co-worker using your curriculum plan at the vocational school, or is a copy in your desk? After you prepare your inventory, organize all the pieces you plan to use in one location.

   B. For indirect documentation, make a list of all the people who could potentially serve to document your knowledge and abilities. Be as thorough as possible. If you own a small business, you might initially think only of your partner. But what about your attorney, your tax accountant or your banker? Often two or three letters from different sources that verify the same aspect of your knowledge prove complementary to one another. One writer may emphasize somewhat different aspects of your knowledge or skills than another.

   Gather articles about yourself, program notes listing you as a speaker or performer, or letters of commendation you may have received for outstanding work in a volunteer organization. Add these to your documentation resource materials. They're likely to come in handy.

3. *Request the documentation you need.*

   This process may take time, so begin to gather your direct documentation as soon as you begin work on your portfolio. If you need letters from former teachers, supervisors or co-workers, start assembling your list and find the addresses. (Some schools have form letters they want you to use. If not, see the discussion of requests for documentation on pp. 110–11) If you have paintings, architectural drawings or other pieces of your work out on display or loan, call or write to make arrangements to retrieve them. If the object is too large to retrieve or if it cannot be removed, make arrangements to have high-quality photographs or slides made of your work. In the case of written materials, make sure to have duplicate copies made to include in your portfolio.

4. *When to request documentation.*

Since you will more than likely depend on others to provide you with some of the documentation you need, you want to send your request letters off as soon as possible after you have enrolled in a portfolio course or begun to work with an assessment counselor. Give your document resource persons a deadline of at least two weeks prior to the time you actually will need their letters. (It would be safer to allow four to six weeks.) After a month, you may wish to follow up your written requests with second phone calls — a gentle reminder that your deadline is fast approaching and an offer to provide any information that will make the job easier for them.

5. *Monitor your documentation requests.*

To keep track of your document resources (to whom you've written, who has responded, the location of other kinds of documentation), develop a worksheet similar to that in Appendix G. It will help you to organize your direct and indirect documentation and permit you to see at a glance what you still need to do. It will also help you avoid last minute problems. You will need to know three things:

- for what courses (or areas of competence) you are seeking credit,
- what kind of documentation you need, and
- where you can get that documentation.

In the first column on the left, list the course names or areas of competence for which you are requesting credit. Then fill out the types of documentation you need and, if applicable, the name of the person who will provide it. Note the dates you mail request letters and the dates the answers are received. This will help you place those necessary follow-up calls if more than a month lapses from the time you made your initial request. Finally, to avoid last minute panic, be sure to note *where* each piece of documentation is kept.

To obtain the necessary indirect documentation, begin by contacting each person twice — once by phone or in person and again in writing. Explain why you want the documentation, mention the assessment program and the college or university by name, and discuss how the documentation will help you.

Content of Letters of Documentation

Letters of documentation may be from former employers, supervisors, teachers — anyone who has been in a position to know you and judge your work. Remember that it is sometimes very difficult for people to understand the difference between a letter of recommendation (which they may have written dozens of times before) and a letter of documentation (which is probably a new concept for most people). You are not asking anyone to verify your character or attest to your winning personality. You are asking the people you contact to confirm that you have indeed done what you claim to have done (worked for ACME widgets for six years from 1978 to 1984), doing the tasks you have said you did, and, most important, demonstrating the learnings you are claiming.

Specify exactly what knowledge you want documented, because only documentation that verifies learning can be used to support your claims as to what you know. A letter intended to document learnings should include:

1. Evidence that the person writing the letter is in a position to be knowledgeable about you and the quality of your work or performance. The letterhead, if it includes the person's title, may be sufficient to convey this. If not, the writer should state in what capacity he knew you, e.g., "I was Jeff's supervisor for five years in the Acme Widget Factory," or "Jeff and I worked together for six months on the Township's planning committee."

2. A detailed summary of your responsibilities or a job description.

3. An explanation of what skills, competencies or knowledge you had to demonstrate in order to fulfill the job responsibilities.

4. An evaluation of your performance on the job, with some indication, if possible, of how that performance might compare with that demanded in a college course. (This last is the most difficult for most people to write, and you may find that you will have to forego this kind of evaluative comment.)

Content of Letters Requesting Documentation

The sample letter below, Exhibit 7-4, which Dorene sent to her supervisor, may be helpful as a model for your own requests. You will want to revise it to fit your personality and make it specific to your needs and circumstances. The more specific you are, the better your chances of getting the document you need.

Sample Letters of Documentation

Some of the answers you receive to your requests for documentation may be fine, others may miss the mark. Following are some samples of both types (Exhibits 7-5, 7-6).

Exhibit 7-5 is not an acceptable letter for Max's portfolio because Mr. Kirchner is giving a character reference, which attests to Max's punctuality, diligence, and generosity in filling in for other employees but says nothing about Max's skills and knowledge.

After receiving this letter, Max went to visit Mr. Kirchner and took the time to explain why he needed a different kind of letter and what kinds of information it should contain (he did not tell Mr. Kirchner what to say). Mr Kirchner's second letter is shown in Exhibit 7-6.

While Exhibit 7-6 is not a perfect letter of validation, it is certainly much better than Mr. Kirchner's first attempt. It does address Max's competence as a projectionist and gives information about his knowledge of film. By itself, however, it could probably not serve as documentation for the six credits Max is asking for in film history and theory since it does not specify the depth and breadth of his knowledge. Although this letter will definitely be included in Max's portfolio, his college will probably also arrange for him to be evaluated by a professor in the film division of the art department.

Dorene G. decided to ask her former employer, Ms. Brown, for a letter that would verify her capabilities in computer applications. She not only wrote her a letter of request (see above), she took the time to make an appointment with Ms. Brown and spent

Exhibit 7-4: Dorene's Letter to Her Supervisor

Ms. Helen Brown, Personnel
A&B Communications, Inc.
125 Main Street, Suite 108
Unionville, AR 55555

Dear Ms. Brown:

As we discussed on the telephone, I am writing to ask you for a letter on my behalf for Unionville College's Portfolio-Assisted Assessment Program. As you know, I am hoping to earn college credits toward my degree for knowledge acquired outside the college classroom. Your letter will help me provide evidence that the knowledge and skills I possess are worthy of college credit.

Following the recommendations specified by the Assessment Program of the college. I would appreciate your writing the letter on company letter-head and including the following:

1. A description of my position with all pertinent past and present experiences included.

2. A mention of your relationship to me (supervisor) and the situations in which you have observed me. Also, please include the dates of your observations and the length of time I worked with you.

3. An indication of my competence, skills and knowledge in word processing, spreadsheets, accounting programs and computer programming. [Here you would specify what your own competencies, skills, and knowledge areas are, and relate them to the course descriptions for which you are seeking credit.]

4. Evaluate how well I performed, using such adjectives as *average, above average, exceptional,* etc. It would also be helpful if your statement included some comparison with others you have known who possess a college degree or college credits and who have held similar positions to mine.

It is important for me to add that what you write should not be a letter of recommendation per se. Rather, the Assessment Program requires that you verify my specific skills, competencies, and knowledge and evaluate the level of my performance.

I would appreciate your sending this letter to my advisor [name] at Unionville College [address]. I would like this letter to reach the advisor no later than [allow at least one month from date you write letter].

Thank you very much for agreeing to write this letter on my behalf. As I am sure you are aware, earning a college degree at this point in my life is very important to me. If you have questions, please let me know.

Sincerely,

Dorene Diaz Garfield

Exhibit 7-5: An Unacceptable Letter
(Written at Max's Telephoned Request)

Detroit Center Theater
180 Lake Drive
Detroit, Michigan 55555-5555
(555) 555-5555

Dear Assessment Counselor:

I am writing this letter for Max Anthony, who worked in my
movie theatre for a number of years as a projectionist.

Max was a fine employee who was always on time and did
whatever he was asked. He would work extra shifts if someone
was ill, and even filled in for the cashier or usher if necessary.

I am certain that Max will succeed in whatever work he attempts
because he is very smart and tries his best at whatever he is
doing.

Sincerely,

Jacob Kirchner

Exhibit 7-6: An Acceptable Letter

Detroit Center Theater
180 Lake Drive
Detroit, Michigan 55555-5555
(555) 555-5555

Dear Assessment Counselor:

Max Anthony worked for me from 1979 to 1984 as projectionist at my movie theatre. During this time, he learned not only to load and service the projector but also assumed the responsibility for all basic maintenance. When we decided to replace our aging projector, I took Max with me because he was so knowledgeable about the various models and capabilities of projectors that I would not have been able to buy one without his help.

I realized after Max had been working for me for a few months that he shared my love of the movies. He began asking my permission to screen old, classical movies when the theatre was closed, and I would frequently find him reading film books and journals. Eventually, he knew more about directors and film history than I did and got my permission to run a foreign film festival on Thursday nights. This turned out to be so well attended that the following year he put together a "History of American Film" festival that ran for 12 weeks and made more money than our regular features. We used to play a kind of trivia game in which we would spring questions about films at each other, but he almost always won.

I keep kidding Max that anytime he gets tired of making automobiles, he should come back and be my projectionist. He was the best I ever had.

Sincerely,

Jacob Kirchner

about half an hour describing the assessment process and explaining why a letter from her would be a crucial document for Dorene's portfolio. Ms. Brown's letter is shown in Exhibit 7-7.

Her letter was not only accepted by the college as adequate documentation for Dorene's computer applications skills, it was used as a sample for the model portfolio that the assessment counselor was putting together. The letter accomplishes the following:

1. It explains Ms. Brown's relationship with Dorene and why she was in a position to be able to document her learnings;

2. it gives a detailed description of those learnings; and

3. it attempts to equate Dorene's learnings with what would be taught in the average college course.

The Problem of Knowledge or Competence Without Documentation

There are many areas of knowledge for which people wish to earn college credit but have no documentation of any sort — direct or indirect. Frequent examples are proficiency in languages or the humanities, such as specialized areas of literature, history or philosophy. A person may have done extensive reading and study, but doesn't know how to prove it. A reading list, though useful, cannot in itself serve as documentation. In these cases, if a student has no documentation and if there are no standardized credit-by-examination opportunities in his or her area of expertise, colleges will frequently arrange for a special evaluation by a selected faculty member in the field. Indeed, many colleges routinely insist on a faculty evaluation of any knowledge or skill for which there is no transcript or recognized authority, even if you have adequate documentation.

Faculty evaluators are chosen because their areas of specialization cover the knowledge or skills for which you are requesting credit. They may assess your knowledge through an interview (formal or informal), an oral examination, a written examination, or a combination of these methods. The results of this evaluation will take the place of documentation in your portfolio. Similarly, if you

Exhibit 7-7: An Excellent Letter

A&B Communications, Inc.
125 Main Street, Suite 108
Unionville, AR 55555
(555) 555-5555

To whom it may concern:

I was Dorene Garfield's immediate supervisor at A&B Communications for four years. During that time I watched Dorene grow from a novice with the computer to one who could handle almost any task we set for her.

Dorene didn't even know word processing when she came to work, but with the help of a manual and some coaching she became proficient first in WordStar and later in Word Perfect. Eventually she could handle any length or kind of document, could do footnotes, make intricate formatting changes and even put the company's enormous mailing system on mail merge. Dorene also taught herself desktop publishing so that she could do our brochures and personnel announcements. A&B began to get a reputation among its competitors as having the best looking direct mail advertising in the business.

Dorene took a company-sponsored course in Lotus 1-2-3 and then designed a new spreadsheet system for the company. Aware that our billing and accounting procedures were too cumbersome, she advised us to buy a new program, Peachtree, and set up our entire accounts receivable and billing processes on this new program. She taught the bookkeeper to use Peachtree and wrote the data entry protocols that enabled us to switch from our old system to the new.

Dorene became thoroughly familiar with the DOS 3.3 system in use in our office and could do simple programming in Basic.

Based on my own experience in teaching a one-year (six-credit) college course in office technologies (State College, 1985), I would say that Dorene's knowledge far exceeds that which is usually covered in a full year in the classroom and that her skills go well beyond what most of the students in my class attained.

Sincerely,

Helen Brown

are seeking credit in an area such as the performing arts or laboratory science, or counseling, you may be expected to undergo a performance evaluation. In any of these cases, speak with someone in the assessment program about your options; there are many ways to get the credit you deserve.

A Word of Caution

Avoid overkill. When assembling documentation, don't succumb to the temptation to clean your attic. If you have to deliver your portfolio in a wheelbarrow, you've overdone it. Be discriminating in what you include as documentation, using only those pieces of evidence which are directly connected to your credit request. For instance, you may have edited the church newspaper for 10 years, but the assessor doesn't have the time to wade through your bound volume of 120 issues of the newspaper. You should present a letter from a church official capable of validating your work and evaluating your editing capacity and perhaps one or two sample editions of the paper in which your name is listed as editor. Portfolios filled with bits and pieces of scrapbook items from a person's entire life not only take too long to read, they tend to be confusing and may work against, rather than for you.

Determining Your Credit Request

One of your toughest tasks in the assessment process is to figure out how much credit it is appropriate to request. Fortunately, you will most likely have a lot of help in doing this from the assessment counselor or other officials in the college responsible for helping you assemble your portfolio. The following approaches are commonly used, although you must find out which your school prefers to make certain you are on the right track.

College Course Method

If your college or the program in which you are enrolled requires you to match your knowledge to specific college courses, much of the burden of requesting the right amount of credit will be lifted from your shoulders. A quick perusal of that college's catalog will show you how much credit is awarded when you successfully complete the courses that most closely approximate what you have learned. If you believe you can demonstrate comparable knowledge through the assessment process, you should request a like amount of credit.

Matching courses to learnings is not always easy, however. What you've learned on your own may not quite fit the way learning is divided into courses. For example, let us suppose you have a great deal of practical experience in installing and repairing electrical appliances, have worked alongside an electrician in wiring your new home, and have assembled and customized your own stereo system. Here is a typical description of a course in general electricity:

General Electricity: 3 credits
Studies basic principles of electricity, laws, theories, devices, instruments and testing equipment. Emphasizes direct and alternating current circuits and devices. An examination of electron theory, resistance, inductance, and capacitance allows the student to analyze and generalize as to the behavior and characteristics of electric current. Laboratory experiences allow students to experiment and apply their learnings to problem-solving situations.

You must ask yourself honestly whether you have the theoretical knowledge implicit in this description. Perhaps you estimate you know about two thirds of the course content. Some colleges would allow you to explain that in the portfolio and ask for two credits rather than three. Or perhaps you are confident that you know everything but capacitance. You might consider reviewing a textbook on electronics and studying the section on capacitance before submitting your portfolio. Or you might consider other possibilities, like adjusting your title from general electricity to practical electronics and adjusting your description to more accurately reflect your learnings.

It is also important to learn whether or not your institution limits the kinds of courses for which you may earn credit. The questions below will help you to gather this information:

Must the courses selected for assessment be from your institution's catalog?

If the descriptions can be from other college catalogs, are there particular limitations or restrictions you need to know?

Can the courses presented for assessment be in your major area, or does the college limit credits earned through prior learning assessment to non-major or free elective areas?

Is there a limit on the number of credits or courses you can earn through assessment of your prior learning?

Can you request credit for an advanced level of a subject area if you have not received credit for the basic or introductory level?[4]

Is there a limit on the number of credits or courses you can earn through assessment of your prior learning?[5]

Let's see how some of the people in the case histories managed to equate their learnings to college courses. Joan B's learnings were relatively easy to state in college course terms because most of the ones she wanted to use in her degree program were traditional in nature. Her list looks like this:

Art

Introduction to Art History (based on formal training at the art museum and years of learning through museum attendance): 6 credits

Egyptian Art and Culture (acquired from independent study for research paper): 3 credits

Elementary Film Making (experiential learning while making film about artists in the city): 3 credits

4. This question sometimes arises in professional fields where a person may know in depth a subject that is ordinarily taught at an advanced level but has not yet learned all of the basic material that is commonly thought of as prerequisite. Some schools have solved this by agreeing to award the advanced credit only after the introductory course has been satisfactorily completed or by retitling the assessed learning and recommending the subsequent completion of the basic course. Since this is usually a faculty issue, our advice is to go ahead and make the credit claim and, if it turns out to be a problem, let the faculty solve it.
5. If there is a limit, and you have enough potential credits to exceed that limit, you will have to make decisions about which of your learnings are the most important in terms of fulfilling requirements for your degree or reflecting on your transcript what you think are your most significant accomplishments.

Communications

Public speaking (based on learning gained from lecturing at the museum): 2 credits

Social Work

Substance abuse counseling (from experience with alcoholic husband and through reading and involvement with Alcoholics Anonymous): 3 credits

Group therapy (from reading and experience with Al Anon): 3 credits

Total Request: 20 credits

Scott A.'s learnings were somewhat more difficult to fit into categories that meshed with his local community college's courses. With the help of his assessment counselor, he realized that what he had learned as a stock boy in a grocery store, while useful to a youngster as a first work experience, was not comparable with what colleges teach and, moreover, had nothing to do with his current educational and career plans. Those learnings, although they were important at a particular time in his life, were eliminated from his assessment list.

Since Scott wants to go into a two-year degree program in forestry, many of the learnings from his years with the paper company are relevant. The head of the department agreed that the experience gained from his years of work in the field were equivalent to the program's requirement of a six-credit field placement, or practicum, and could be assessed for credit as such, but in addition he is requesting credit for three courses in the forestry curriculum.

The director of the physical education department said that although the school does not currently give a course in fishing, she would be willing to consider Scott's expertise in that area as a substitute for the physical education requirement if his learnings could be validated through a performance evaluation by a faculty member.

According to the college catalog, the English department did not offer a course in the literature of the Bible, but the religion and philosophy department did, so Scott has placed his learnings under titles that will be submitted to that department. He understands that simply demonstrating his factual knowledge of the Old and New Testaments is not enough; he must also show that he understands them on the levels of literature, myth, metaphor, and history; as textual accretion; and as primary religious and philosophical sources for the Judeo-Christian tradition.

The art department agreed to consider Scott's furniture making as a craft for which they could possibly award credit, but the college had no category under which his skills at carpentry and wood working could be assessed.

So far, Scott's list of potential learnings for his portfolio looks like this:

Forestry

Operation of and maintenance of heavy machinery (bull dozer, tractor, log hauler, skidder, etc.): 3 credits

Field Logging Operations: A Practicum: 6 credits

The Ecology of Forest Maintenance: 3 credits

The Technology of Paper Making: 3 credits

Physical Education

Fishing as a sport: 1 credit

Religion and Philosophy

The Literature of the Old and New Testaments: 3 credits

Leadership techniques for Bible study: 2 credits

Arts and Crafts

Furniture design, making and refinishing: 6 credits

Total Request: 27 credits

Dorene's list:

Computer Science

Basic computer literacy: 3 credits

Office technologies: 9 credits

Labor Relations

History of labor relations in the United States: 2 credits

Labor negotiations and arbitration: 2 credits

Modern Languages

Beginning and intermediate Spanish: 6 credits

Latin American literature and culture: 3 credits

Political Science

History and analysis of the Puerto Rican statehood movement: 3 credits

Total Request: 28 credits

Anna's list:

Psychology

Basic child psychology: 3 credits

Early childhood growth and development: 3 credits

Practicum in child care: 3 credits

Business

Management of non-profit organizations: 3 credits

Personnel management: 3 credits

Public relations: 3 credits

Financial management: 3 credits

Culinary Arts

Basic principles of cooking and baking: 6 credits

Ethnic cuisines: 3 credits

Total Request: 30 credits

Learning Components Method

Learning components is an educational phrase that refers to what you know and what you can do. It permits you to cluster your learning in the way you know it, rather than in the way college courses categorize and describe knowledge. Earlier we mentioned that experiential learning is sometimes messy, that it doesn't fall into neat packages like college courses. Some institutions cope with this dilemma by encouraging individuals to cluster knowledge and skills by listing the specific skills, competencies, and accomplishments that reflect college level-learning.

Suppose, for example, that you know something about writing:

■ you have worked in an office and know how to write business letters and memos;

■ as part of your work with a volunteer agency, you regularly write press releases; and

■ Last year you had a children's story published in a local magazine.

It is highly unlikely that you would find any one course in business, journalism or creative writing to describe your knowledge and skill as a writer. In such a case you could cluster your learnings by listing your specific skills, competencies and accomplishments. For example, you know how to:

■ gather information;
■ determine the important points;
■ write simply and convincingly;
■ tailor your writing to the audience and purpose;
■ create imaginary characters; and
■ handle narrative and point of view

And you have considerable documentation to prove it. Your next step is to translate these learning components into some number of college credits. Upon consultation with the assessment counselor or a professor in the English department, you might be encouraged to request six credits for your writing competencies, three for the equivalent of a freshman writing course and three for an advanced writing course.

Using a College Catalog

One way to translate learning components into numbers of college credits is to "informally" use a written college course description (or a set of them, as in the college catalog). Although you may not be required to equate your knowledge to a specific course, the descriptions can be helpful. If you already have experience taking college courses and know in general what is expected in a standard three credit-hour course, you're one step ahead. For example, you took a course in principles of accounting last year and earned three credit-hours. Now in your portfolio you are requesting credit in banking. You might assign a credit-hour value to your banking knowledge by recalling what was required to earn the credits in accounting. Perhaps you will only want to request two credits, or three or four, or even six, based on your recollection of the effort and content of a typical course.

College catalogs may also be used to compare your level of knowledge to that detailed in the course descriptions. As you read a particular description, ask yourself: do I *know* that, am I able to *do* that, is that what my *evidence* reflects? Estimate the percent of knowledge you think you have for each course that touches on your areas of expertise.

While course descriptions vary from being very informative and detailed to quite sketchy, they are the most readily available sources of information. They can give you clues to what college faculty expect you to know in a particular field and are excellent tools that should be taken advantage of on your way to a degree.

Using the Carnegie Formula

There is a second method of assigning a credit value to learning components that may be particularly useful if your knowledge was acquired through noncredit courses or workshops sponsored by such organizations as churches, businesses and unions. The Carnegie Formula is a time ratio typically used by colleges in the United States to calculate college course credit. A standard three credit-hour course requires students to spend 45 hours of class time and 90 hours of out-of-class work in order to receive credit. In other words, for every 15 hours of instruction and 30 hours of preparation, you earn one credit hour.

For example, suppose you attended a business management seminar sponsored by a major manufacturing company. The group met for six hours each week for five weeks, totalling 30 hours of time in the seminar. You estimate that you spent an additional 60 hours doing assignments and the required readings. With sufficient evidence to support your claim to credit (a course syllabus, a list of readings and assignments, a document indicating you had indeed been enrolled in the course and passed it), you might want to request two credit hours. Alternatively, if the course is listed in the *ACE Guide*, most colleges will simply accept the guide's credit recommendation.

Help From Your College

No matter what method you use to calculate your credit request, as in all the other decisions you will make in preparing for assessment, you can and should expect the college to help you. Such help may come in the form of a portfolio workshop or of advice and assistance made available to you through an assessment counselor or member of the faculty.

Organizing Your Portfolio

You've assembled your list of learnings, related them to subjects taught in college, documented them, determined the amount of credit you will request and written your essay or narrative. Now you are ready to put your portfolio together. It would be helpful if there were a single universal model portfolio to follow, but unfortunately there is not. Each institution has its own requirements, though some leave the final structure and organization of the portfolio up to the student.

The basic principle that should guide you in putting together your portfolio is this: *make it easy for the reader to understand*. Remember that your readers are busy people, college faculty and administrators, for whom reading your portfolio is only one of many, many tasks they must accomplish in a typical day. Your portfolio should be:

■ *Selective*. Only those facts, learnings, documents, and data which are directly connected with your credit request should be included in the portfolio. Avoid redundancy.

- *Logically organized.* The plan or arrangement of the document should enable your readers to follow your thinking as they go from section to section. This means that you should keep your terminology consistent (don't call the same thing "business studies" in one section and "office procedures" in another) and keep things in the same order. If your learnings are listed chronologically in one place, don't switch to an alphabetical or order of importance listing in another without clear explanation.

- *Coherent — the connections among the parts should be understandable.* Each section should be tied to the others with brief transitional statements or explanations if necessary, and the reader should never have to stop to question why you are bringing in an idea or information at a specific time.

- *Neat, grammatically correct, and clearly written.* The portfolio should look and read like a document worthy of a competent college student. Ideally it should be done through word processing for appearance and ease of revision. If you must settle for typing, that's fine, but edit carefully. Don't submit a handwritten document.

Despite the lack of a universal portfolio format, there are several elements that nearly all portfolio requirements have in common. The following elements give the portfolio coherence and connectivity:

Cover Page

This should identify your institution and the name of the assessment program in which you are enrolled. It should also contain your name, address, and phone number and include the date that you are submitting the portfolio. (See the sample portfolio cover page in Exhibit 7-8.)

Table of Contents

As in any book, the table of contents gives readers an overview of the organization of the portfolio and guides them to each of its sections. You may wish to do a first draft of a table of contents early on and use it as an outline to what you plan to include.

Exhibit 7-8: Sample Portfolio Cover Page

PORTFOLIO FOR PRIOR LEARNING ASSESSMENT
submitted to
UNIONVILLE COLLEGE

ADULT ACCESS PROGRAM

by
DORENE DIAZ GARFIELD

November 6, 1992

2315 High Street
Starr City, AR 55555
(717) 663-4768

Then, when you are ready to put the whole document together, revise the table of contents to correspond to any changes in your organization of material, and, finally, add the correct page numbers.

Essay or Narrative

This part provides the assessor with a picture of who you are. As described earlier, the essay or narrative should show the relationship between your learning experiences and your college-level knowledge in the context of your life and educational goals. If, in the course of your work on this portfolio, you have also discovered some areas in which your present learning is inadequate and you intend to study further, this is information that your assessors should have. What is important is that you explain how your learnings relate to the further study you intend to pursue.

Learning Components, Competency Statements or Course Descriptions, and Their Documentation in Each Learning Area Presented

This is the heart of most portfolios. It should identify each learning component or course for which you are seeking credit and provide the supporting documentation or evidence. It should also specify the number of credits you are seeking. For clarity's sake, this section should be preceded by a list of all the learning components, the documentation being submitted, and the credit request. A sample from Dorene G.'s portfolio is shown in Exhibit 7-9.

Following this list in Dorene's portfolio is a one-page competency statement for each area of learning (in the order in which they appear in the list), including the source of the learning and a detailed description of precisely what she has learned and/or can do, with the credit request on the bottom of the page and the documentation immediately following. Each item of documentation (transcripts, letters, certificates) has been marked in such a way as to connect it to the learning component it addresses. Thus, Dorene has printed a large "C" in the upper right-hand corner of the certificate for union course #410, so the reader can easily

**Exhibit 7-9: List of Learning Components,
Their Documentation and Credits Requested**

Learning Component	Documentation	Requested Credits Requested
A. Basic computer literacy	Letter from employer	3*
B. Office technologies	PSI certifying exam Letter from employer	9*
C. History of labor relations in U.S.	Certificate of participation in union course #410 Facsimile of American Council on Education's credit recommendation for course #410	2
D. Labor negotiations and arbitration	Letter from union representative testifying to participation in process and level of competency	2*
E. Beginning and intermediate Spanish	CLEP test transcript	6
F. History of the Puerto Rican statehood movement	Letter from Dr. A. Haines, political science department, Unionville College, testifying to level of competency	3
G. South American literature and culture	Letter from Dr. K. Watts, modern languages department, Unionville College, testifying to level of competency	3

Total Request: 28 credits

*To be applied to major in business studies

identify the learning component to which it refers, an "F" on the letter from Dr. Haines, and so on. Although this attention to detail may seem unnecessary, it is critical if readers are to be able to find their way around your portfolio, understand it, and make decisions about the merit of your credit request.

Submitting Your Portfolio

Remember, neatness counts. For some of the people who read it, the portfolio will be all they will ever know of you. If they must struggle with sloppy handwriting or poorly typed pages, they will associate their discomfort with the kind of person they suppose you to be. And if the manuscript is full of typos, misspellings or grammatical errors, they will have a difficult time divorcing their negative response to the language skills demonstrated in the portfolio from the other learnings you claim to have. Keep in mind that college-level knowledge, regardless of the subject area, assumes a basic competence in communication, writing in particular.

Revise and revise until the manuscript is as perfect as you can make it. Always have someone else check your work one last time for errors that you may have missed. If you are using word processing, be sure to take advantage of spelling- or grammar-checking programs available.

Once you have assembled your portfolio and checked it one more time for completeness and accuracy, make a duplicate copy for your own records before submitting the original to the appropriate college office.[6] If some of your documentation (such as photographs, letters or publications with your name on them) is valuable to you, ask if the school would be willing to accept copies rather than originals. For safety, these copies can be put in plastic envelopes designed for three-ring binders.

---

6. The use of a three-ring binder, sized for standard-sized typing paper, (8½×11) is convenient and enables you to make changes and rearrange pages as necessary. Standard dividers, sold in any stationery store, can be used to mark the divisions of the portfolio (essay, documentation, etc.), making it easier for the reader/assessor to locate information.

The day you hand in your portfolio you will probably experience an enormous sense of relief. When you submit evidence of your prior learning, you are also submitting a large piece of yourself, quite beyond the physical contents of your portfolio. This takes self-confidence, a high degree of motivation, and a willingness to take risks — surely the keys to success in any endeavor.

Faculty Evaluation

Only one more hurdle remains: the actual assessment of your portfolio. In some colleges, the portfolio is assessed by a committee of faculty or faculty and administrators. It becomes their task to read the entire document; to weigh the evidence of learning; to make judgments as to whether that learning has the appropriate breadth, depth and theoretical basis to make it comparable with what you might have learned from similar college courses; to see if the documentation matches and supports the learning; to make certain there is no overlap (for example, a request for credit for writing that looks similar to transcript credit for a freshman English course); to see how the learning fits into the student's degree program and overall education and career planning; and, finally, to weigh the credit request against the evidence of learning to see whether the request is reasonable.

Occasionally this process of assessment goes on without any further involvement on your part. More frequently, however, the assessment office will make an appointment with you to speak to faculty in some or all of your areas of learning, so that they may evaluate that learning in a face-to-face interview. This interview may be conducted as a casual conversation or as a more formal oral examination, but in either case its purpose is evaluative, that is, to see if your discussion of what you know matches up with what you have presented in your portfolio.

The faculty interview is not something to be dreaded. If yours is a strong portfolio presentation, the faculty person may simply want to confirm that you and your portfolio "match." Or the faculty person may wish to question you on something that was not quite clear, or may wish to find out whether what looked weak in your presentation arose from lack of knowledge or inadequate presentation of that knowledge.

Some students prepare for their faculty evaluations by reviewing a standard textbook that covers their experientially gained knowledge. This is useful if you think you want to brush up on the vocabulary, or jargon, of a particular area or if you want to refresh your memory of theory or specific facts.

In any case, you needn't dread the faculty evaluation. It will almost always be a benign procedure: fair, reasonable, and humanely conducted. Its purpose is to find out what you *do know*, not what you don't. In fact, the outcome of some faculty evaluations is a recommendation that the student's credit request should be *raised*.

The Transcript

After your portfolio is assessed and the credit awards recommended, you, the registrar, and sometimes the dean will be notified of the results.

The registrar is the college official who prepares students' transcripts — records of their progress and achievement in the college. It is the registrar's duty to record on your transcript the amount of credit you have earned through the portfolio process and to break it down into courses or learning components. The transcript becomes a document that follows you throughout life. If you wish to transfer credits to another college, if you wish to apply for graduate school, or if you are applying for a job for which you need proof of credits or a degree, the transcript is the official document that you must produce.

A few weeks after the completion of assessment, you may wish to ask the registrar's office for a copy of your transcript so you can check its accuracy and make certain that everything is in order.

Completion of the Process

You have done it! You have taken a lifetime of experience and turned it into a coherent account of the learnings produced by that experience. Whether you have earned six credits or 60, you have proven that you are an accomplished adult learner. You should feel a great sense of pride in your accomplishment and should look to your future in college with renewed anticipation of reward and satisfaction.

In the next chapter, we will look at some of the issues you will face as you add being a student to your already crowded list of activities and responsibilities. And we will discuss some strategies for coping with the demands of going back to school.

8

Surviving & Thriving in College

"I have but one lamp by which my feet are guided, and that is the lamp of experience."
—Patrick Henry

OK, this is it. You're going to be a student again. You've explored your career and life goals, you know what you want to do when you "grow up." You have identified the school that most closely meets your needs, have applied and been accepted, have talked to the assessment counselor and perhaps even registered for a prior learning assessment workshop, and have chosen the first course or courses you'll take. Suddenly, you're getting nervous. You're wondering again if it's going to be too hard for you to manage, if you'll be able to keep up with the others in your class, whether you have the ability to write a paper or take a test or the courage to speak out when the professor asks for discussion.

Of course, lots of things would be different if you were 18 years old. Most of your friends would probably be starting college with you, and you could kid each other about being nervous and unsure. You'd be doing what everyone else would expect you to do at that age, and you wouldn't have to juggle a job and home responsibilities and maybe even children. But if you were 18 years old you wouldn't have all your valuable experience, and you wouldn't have such a clear sense of *why* you're taking this step and what you expect to get from it. You also probably wouldn't have the commitment that enables adult students to do so well when they return to the classroom.

If you were 18 years old, your mother might take you to the mall to buy you new shoes or a sweater and a nifty briefcase. Why don't you do it for yourself? Treat yourself! Celebrate! You're embarking on a great adventure, and it's going to be fun.

Getting the Feel of the Campus

You'll be a lot more comfortable about going back to school if you don't wait until the first night of class to figure out in which building your course is meeting, how to get into the parking lot, or where the bookstore is. By now you should have talked to friends or co-workers who have gone to your college and read the college catalog, but some kinds of information about the way a school "feels" are not readily available, either from people or printed information. To get a real sense of a school, you should probably take yourself on a campus tour. Talk to students as well as school officials, look over the library, the bookstore, the cafeterias or student hang outs, perhaps even sit in on a class or two. You may feel more comfortable if you go with your spouse or a friend. You may even find one or two people at work who will join you.

When you visit the campus, choose the time of day during which you will be attending class. Find each of the following locations, and *while you are there*, if possible, answer each of the following questions in your notebook.

Getting There

- How long did it take you to drive (or take the bus or train) from your home to the campus? Or from work to the campus? Did you travel in a time of heavy or light traffic? Is your class scheduled in a time of heavy or light traffic? How much time will you need to allow yourself to be sure that you get to class on time?

- Where did you park? Is there a lot reserved for students? Do you need a special parking pass or sticker to get into the lot? Where can you obtain such a pass? What will it cost?

- In what building is your class scheduled? How far from the parking lot or bus stop is the building? How long will it take you to walk to your classroom building?

The Library

- Find the library. Go inside and look around. Find:
    - the card catalog;
    - "stacks" where books are shelved;
    - the section where current magazines and journals are kept;
    - the "reserve" book shelves where books that instructors have reserved for their students are kept;
    - the research section where dictionaries, encyclopedias, periodical indexes and other research tools are available;
    - the audiovisual section, where you can view or listen to videotapes, films, and records; and
    - computers and typewriters for student use.

- How is the library being used? What are people actually doing?

- Would you feel comfortable reading, studying and doing research here?

- Ask one of the librarians what the hours of the library are, where you would find books in your field, and for how long a period books can be borrowed.

- Do you need a special library card to use the library, or is your college registration card sufficient?

- Is there an orientation tour of the library for new students? If so, sign up for it now.

Remember, the college library will be a critical resource for you, regardless of your field. The librarian's most important job is to help students, and you should take full advantage of that help in locating the printed and audiovisual materials you need, doing research, and utilizing the library's other services.

Other College Offices

- Where is the dean of students office, the admissions office, the registrar's office, the study skills center, and the prior learning assessment office?

- What hours are each of these places open?

- Where is your instructor's office? Are regular office hours posted when he or she will be available?

In Classes & Between

- Observe the students emerging from class. Are they talking to one another? Do they seem enthusiastic about their studies?

- Peek into a few classrooms just as class is letting out. Are there students staying behind to talk with the professor? Does he or she seem friendly and helpful?

- Where do students go to hang out? Is there a cafeteria, a student lounge, a place where people seem to gather informally?

- How does the atmosphere of these places seem to you — friendly, reserved, boisterous and noisy?

- Are there other people of your age group? Gender? Ethnic background?

■ Are most of the students dressed casually or do they seem dressed up? Is this a jeans- and-sneakers or a jacket-and-tie campus?

The more you can find out about the campus before you start class, the more relaxed you will be. The campus tour is a great way to prepare yourself for your new adventure.

Managing Your Time

If you asked most working adults what is most precious to them (after their friends and family), they would probably say time. None of us seem ever to have enough time to perform our paid jobs responsibly, take care of our families and homes, pay attention to our health and grooming needs, engage in community and social activities, and still go out to a ball game, play poker, read the newspaper or just "veg out." Now you're thinking about going back to school, and you're wondering how you're going to fit it all in.

First, let's look at how much time school is actually likely to take. There's the class time, of course — roughly three hours per week if you're taking a three-credit course. And then the two hours of reading and study that are theoretically needed to support each hour of classroom time — which for a three-credit course adds up to nine hours per week. (That number could be lower at some points in the semester, but could increase around exam time or when papers are due.)

But what about commuting time to and from the campus? And incidental time, like that spent seeing a counselor, tracking down your records in the registrar's office, having an appointment with your professor, working on your assessment portfolio or just sitting down over coffee to talk to the guy who sits next to you in chemistry? Conservatively speaking, you should figure that going back to school for just one course will probably cost you at least an additional 12 to 16 hours of your time per week. Where's it going to come from?

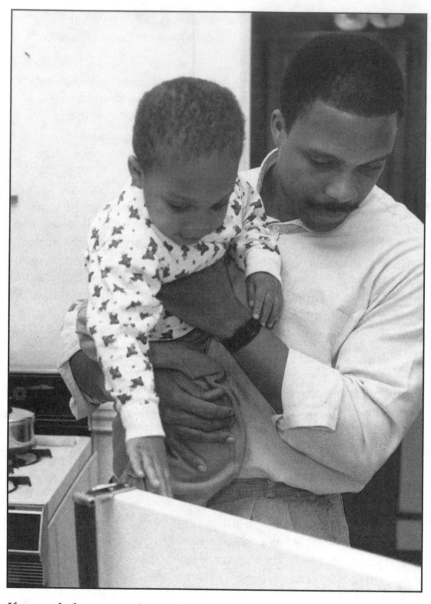

If you asked most working adults what is most precious to them (after their family and friends), they would probably say time. Now you're thinking about going back to school, and you're wondering how you're going to fit it all in!

There are many time management systems, but one of the simplest begins with constructing your own pie chart, finding out how you're currently spending your time so that you can begin to think about reallocating it. Look at the four circles in Exercise 8-1. Each is divided into 24 hours—and you can't have more than that no matter how clever you are. Think about that 24 hours. How much sleep must you have in order to function well—six hours? seven? eight? And how much time do you work at your job per day? 9 hours? plus commuting? What about taking care of your home, your children, the dog? Preparing and eating meals? Getting dressed? Calling your friends and relatives? Watching television? Fill in the top left circle of Exercise 8-1 with an approximation of how you now spend your allotted 24 hours during the week. Then fill in the top right circle for your weekends—good news, you may be able to pick up a few unscheduled hours on the weekends.

If you're like most of us, your first reaction to filling out the pie chart is likely to be that you don't even have time to do the things you're doing now; how can you take on going to school? Well, tens of thousands of adults are already doing it, but there's a cost. You have to be willing to look closely at how you're spending your time now to decide which activities are your real priorities and which could be dropped or turned over to someone else.

The "average" person uses his or her time in this way: sleep, 33 percent; work, 40 percent; maintenance, 15 percent (dressing, cooking, cleaning, etc.); free, 12 percent (depends on family responsibilities).

What is "free" time? It's what's left over after sleep, work and maintenance. It's the approximately 2.88 hours a day that you have to do everything else, whether playing with your kids or having a beer with your friends or listening to your favorite rock group.

In turning to the third and fourth pie charts — your projection of how you will allot your time to accommodate going back to school — you have to make some hard decisions. This brings us to the classic time management system.

Exercise 8-1: The Pie Chart System of Time Management

How I'm Managing My Time Now

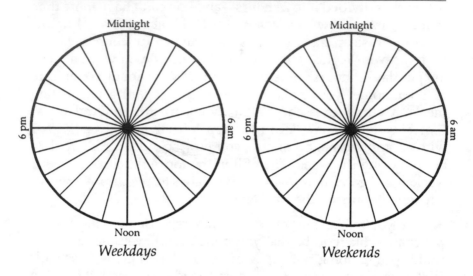

Weekdays   Weekends

How I'll Manage My Time When I'm In School

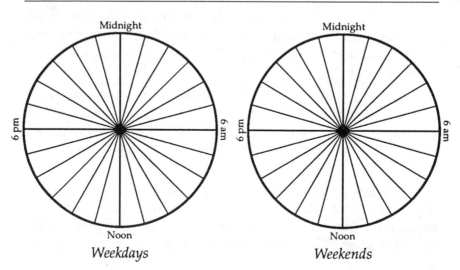

Weekdays   Weekends

Classic Time Management System

All time management plans are based on a simple system of prioritizing tasks into three categories:

A. Very important/must do
B. Maintenance — get them done or they pile up
C. Need doing, but can wait

Which tasks do you think are most popular? You guessed it — "C" tasks: groom the dog, read the sports page, call Aunt Leah in Chicago, watch reruns of "thirtysomething".... Where did the time go?

"C" tasks are fun, low pressure and satisfying to cross off the list. "A" tasks are difficult, important, pressured and carry the risk of failure. The first step is knowing the difference between A, B and C tasks. Get in the habit of sorting out jobs on a daily and weekly basis using this system, and then get the As and as many of the Bs out of the way as you can.

But you're thinking, "I've only got the weekends and about three extra hours a day to do everything!" You're right, and that's why managing your time is a critical issue. You will probably have to give up some of your leisure activities for a while, and you may end up "buying time" from other people — having someone type your papers, a neighborhood youngster mow your lawn, or your children take over feeding and grooming the cat.

Although there are many time management techniques that you may want to learn about, this simple prioritizing method is a good basic tool for getting control of your time. Besides, it's very satisfying to have listed your As, Bs and Cs so you can have the pleasure of crossing them off as you go. Exercise 8-2 will help you get started.

Energy Cycles

Next, figure out your own personal energy cycle. Some people have always been early risers, some night owls. Do you wake up at 5:00 A.M. whistling "Chariots of Fire?" Or are you the type

Exercise 8-2: Prioritizing Tasks

1. On a separate piece of paper, list 20 non-job-related activities that you perform in the course of an average month—anything from weeding and feeding the vegetable garden to having your mother-in-law to dinner to taking the cub scouts to the planetarium. Don't forget the obvious ones like paying bills, doing the laundry, driving Johnny to his karate lessons, and meeting your friends for a movie on Friday nights.

2. Now prioritize these 20 activities as A, B or C.

3. Take a good hard look at your As. Remember, As are must dos. You must make certain that bills are paid, the family doesn't starve, the leak in the plumbing is fixed. But must you actually do all of these? Can you spend less time on them? Can you pay someone else to do them or get a friend or relative to help you out?

4. Look at your Bs and Cs. Which can you cut off the list? Which can you postpone or do less often? Which could somebody else take over? Does your mother-in-law have to come to dinner every week? Maybe she'd enjoy going out for fast food with your family occasionally while you're at school.

5. Look back over your whole list. How many of the 20 activities have you been able to eliminate? How much time have you saved?

that never misses Jay Leno? When are you most energetic and alert? Use that "prime time" for A tasks and save the Bs and Cs for times when you are less alert.

Until you get used to studying, taking notes, going to the library and other new tasks, the whole business will probably take a greater amount of time than when these things are routine. So start out easy and plan ahead. And try to use your high-energy times for your most demanding school work.

Beware the Time Vampires

Time can be stolen away if you're not careful. You won't want to live your entire life in such a careful way, but while you are in school you will need to be stingy about your time. For instance:

- Make an agreement with your housemates about your study time, follow the agreement yourself, and beware of repeat offenders. If your son always chooses your study time to ask for help with homework, sit down and have a little talk about why you are going to school and what it means for the family.

- Stay off the phone. There is no law that you have to answer a telephone. They will call back if it's important. If you do answer the phone, saying "I can't talk now, I'm studying" ought to do it.

- Relax. You have probably established some standards in your life that come out of having enough time to enjoy them. Folded sheets in the cupboard, a well-waxed car or a very tidy lawn are all great when you've got the time. You may temporarily have to slack off on some of these time-consuming activities to accomplish your goal.

- Try to strike a balance between indulging yourself in all the partying, television and baseball you've always enjoyed and denying yourself all pleasurable activities. You don't have to become a self-denying hermit for the next few years, but you probably will have to give up some activities you'll miss.

Clearly, going to school requires that you organize your life better than ever before. You will still feel pressured by such a full schedule, but you can manage if you are thoughtful about how you use your time and resources. You will probably have to give up some fun activities, but keep reminding yourself that you're not giving them up forever and that you're gaining something very important: learning that will empower you and enable you to grow and make important career and personal changes in your life.

Talk openly with your family about this issue. You may be surprised by their willingness to help you tackle this problem.

Creating a Support System

This is a time in your life when you're going to need to shore up your support system. What is a support system? It's the cluster of people in your life that you can count on. The people at work, at home and in your social life who are there when you need them, who will listen to your troubles, who can make you feel good about yourself, who will pitch in and help in an emergency.

Survey your own support system. Think about who you rely on; who you wish you could rely on; who disappoints you more times than helps you. Completing Exercise 8-3 should help.

Exercise 8-3: Surveying Your Support System

List the important people in your life under these categories:

Rooters. These are the people who are excited about your new plan. They will encourage you and give you emotional support.

_____

_____

_____

Constants. These are the people who like you just the way you are and feel a little nervous about how you may change if you go back to school. They're not against the idea, but they don't like the idea of changes, period.

_____

_____

_____ →

Resources. These are the people at work and in school, in the library, wherever, who have the information and services that can make it easier for you.

_____

_____

_____

Challengers. These are the people you look to for guidance and inspiration. They are your advisors, mentors and role models. They may be people who have already done what you want to do, and they can give you good advice as well as encouragement.

_____

_____

_____

Toxics. These are people who put you down and sabotage your efforts because of their own problems. They are people who drain your energy and make you feel uncertain.

_____

_____

_____

I hope your list of rooters is longer than your list of toxics! Don't be surprised if you've listed some of the people in your family in more than one category, including a mix of positives and negatives. Your going to school will definitely affect them, and it is a good idea to keep communication open as you go along.

For example, a husband may be very proud of his wife's going back to school (rooter), but still resent the fact that she's gone two nights a week (toxic). Your Aunt Sarah may offer to help you out by doing the food shopping for you on weekends, but you have the feeling that deep down she thinks you're just complicating your life unnecessarily (constant).

The challenge is to find ways to move those closest to you into positive roles, to turn potential constants and toxics into rooters, resources and challengers. You might want to spend considerable time making certain that your children understand why you're going to school and what positive consequences it will have for all of you as a family when you achieve your goal. If they can understand that you will be in line for a better job at higher pay, or if they can be made to see that your commitment to learning will bring you closer to them while they are also learning in school, or if they are secure in knowing that less time together doesn't mean less love, then they will be better able to tolerate your absences, the lack of home-baked desserts, the many inconveniences of having a parent who is less available to them than before.

It's also a good idea to include your spouse or best friend in some of your new interests and activities when you're going to school. Discuss a great idea you got from your political science course, ask your friend to accompany you to an open lecture on campus, show your spouse how a new accounting procedure might work on the family budget, invite a classmate home to meet your nearest and dearest.

Of course, your support system, no matter how strong, works best if it starts with you. Your confidence that you can make it, your pride in being a lifelong learner, your commitment to what you are doing form the bedrock of your success. Be your own best rooter. Your family has a right to know what they are getting into, and so do you. As part of their preparation for going to school, some adults have negotiated contracts with their families or housemates, spelling out each person's duties, privileges and trade-offs.

Strategies for Negotiating a Contract

For some families, a formal, written contract is a good way of making sure that everyone involved understands what kinds of support you will need in going back to school and what kinds of trade offs there will be. Sitting down to talk this out with parents, spouses, children or the friends with whom you live and then spelling out on paper the agreements reached can be a great way of getting these issues out in the open before they can cause hurt feelings or resentment.

Keep in mind that contracts are a two-way street. Every contract means compromise on both sides. Your family members have a right to their own reasonable demands. If, for example, you play cards two weekday nights and now plan to attend college the other two, of course your family will protest your absence four nights in a row each week. Your understanding response to their concerns (and your willingness to make a few deals) is the best strategy you've got.

Your contract might include some of the following issues:

A. *The quiet clause.* No music will be played in the house from 8:00 to 11:00 P.M.. on Tuesday or Wednesday. In return, Bob and Karen will be allowed to eat dinner in front of the TV on those nights.

B. *The card game clause.* Instead of playing cards two evenings a week (or going to ball games or shopping or visiting friends), Frank will now attend school two evenings a week and play cards once every other week.

C. *The Burger King clause.* Paul will be responsible for feeding the kids on the evenings Mary is in school. He is allowed to take them to Burger King as often as he wishes.

Important note: Only negotiate contract clauses that you are really prepared to live with, and once you've got the contract, keep to it. Subsequent extra nights out or complaints about the lack of nutritional value in fast foods are against the rules.

Max (see profiles, chapter 2, page 18) has a contract with his girlfriend that she will babysit for him three nights a week while he's in class and will type his papers. In return, he has offered to take over the maintenance of her car (a job she hates) and will keep one night a week free so that they can attend dance recitals and go to the theater (her special interests, which Max has always been reluctant to accommodate).

Anna, who is back in school now, has contracted with her youngest son (the only one still at home) to increase his allowance in return for his taking over the family shopping and laundry. Her husband has agreed to clean the house on Saturdays, and they have all agreed that they will forego Anna's superb cooking a few nights a week and go out for inexpensive dinners.

Know Your Family

Your in-depth knowledge of your family's personalities and needs may prove to be the most important factor in getting through the next few years with relationships not only intact but even strengthened. If your wife hates clutter on the kitchen table, set up a card table in the bedroom for studying. If your husband hates not watching evening TV, plan to study in the library a few times a week. If your kids are proud that Mommy or Daddy is going to school too, do your homework together from time to time.

Money Matters

If you're like most adults, you've probably already begun to think about what college will cost, and you've found out that per course or per credit charges vary widely. Although state and locally supported schools may be much less expensive than private colleges and universities, you should not automatically make your decision based on cost. While a community college that charges $50 per credit may seem a real bargain when compared with a college that charges $200 per credit, you owe it to yourself to make certain that your first priority is to choose the school that offers the programs or courses you need. (See chapter 4.) Sometimes the more expensive schools may become affordable through their special scholarships or through a particularly generous financial aid package.

If you're lucky, you work for a company or belong to a union that has education benefits that will cover some or all of the tuition. Some companies advertise their tuition benefits widely; others don't publicize them. Talk to your own company's benefits person to find out what their policy is and if you qualify. Even if you can't get help from your employer, however, there are a number of sources of financial aid that may be available to you. In recent years, with the increasing numbers of adults going back to school, some programs have begun to consider part-time students eligible for aid.

The major kinds of financial aid include:

- *Grants.* These may be from federal, state or college sources and may vary widely in amount, but typically they are tied to financial need and dependent on your being enrolled in an eligible institution and making satisfactory progress in your classes.

- *Loans.* The sources and amounts of loan programs may vary from year to year and program to program, but in general they are made by state and federal governments or by local lending institutions and colleges. They are usually at an interest rate somewhat below that charged for conventional loans.

- *Scholarships.* These vary widely from school to school and from one geographic area to another and may be sponsored by the college or by outside groups with an interest in education. They may cover all or part of tuition costs and may also include stipends for books or housing. Scholarships may be granted on the basis of merit or grade point average or because you belong to a special group (women, minorities, children of people in certain professions, etc.) for which money has been set aside.

- *College work-study.* This is a program jointly sponsored by the college and federal government in which the student is paid for working for the college for a given number of hours per month.

As you can see, financial aid is a complicated subject that varies from one school to another and also changes from year to year as federal and state governments develop new programs to help people go to college. Moreover, students are not necessarily limited to just one kind of tuition aid. It is frequently possible to put together a package of loans and grants or loans and scholarships, depending on the student's financial needs and full or part-time, graduate or undergraduate status.

Don't despair. *Help is available.* Every college has a financial aid officer whose responsibility it is to give you the information you need about the kinds of aid available and to assist you in making applications. Sometimes you will find that the more expensive colleges turn out to be affordable because of the greater variety of financial aids packages they can put together.

While educational benefits may pay for the most expensive part of going to school, tuition and fees, there will be additional costs such as books, school supplies, transportation, parking and snacks. Depending on the course or program in which you are enrolled, books may represent a substantial investment, particularly in some of the technical or professional fields. And some colleges have begun recommending the purchase of a personal computer.

Even without the major cost of a computer, the beginning of each term may require up to $200 in cash. Can you budget ahead for that? It may be useful for you to try to calculate the true cost of returning to school using the items in Exercise 8-4 as your guide.

Developing Good Study Habits

Having a Place to Study

Dorene finds it difficult to study in her apartment with her roommate talking on the phone or listening to music or wanting to talk to her. She goes to the college library after work three nights per week and on Saturdays goes to her local community library for a few hours. She has gotten to know the librarians at both places, and they help her find the information and books she needs. The college library has individual "carrels," small desks where she can read and take notes and leave her books and papers while she is at the card catalog or out for a snack, and she finds

Exercise 8-4: Calculating the Cost of School

Tuition*	_____
Books**	_____
Supplies	_____
Fees*	_____
Household Help	_____
Quick Foods	_____
Transportation	_____
Child Care	_____
Other	_____
Total	_____

*These may be covered by educational benefits.
**Most college bookstores put out the texts ordered for each course a few weeks before class starts. You can estimate the cost of books by finding the section where your course's books are on display and simply adding up the prices. (You could also buy the books early and get a head start on your reading.)

that when she is working at her carrel, her concentration is so intense she loses track of time.

Joan has converted a large closet in her home into a study. She fitted her grandmother's small antique desk into the space, hung her favorite Picasso print above it, installed a strong overhead light, and built open book/storage shelves along one wall with a pull out shelf for her typewriter. Her sons know that when she is in her "study" they are not to call her to the phone or bother her for anything less than a full-scale emergency.

You will need a place to study and store your materials, a place that is comfortable and private, that has good lighting and a minimum of distracting clutter.

Max can concentrate anywhere, anytime. Because he doesn't want his children to feel excluded by his studying, he has set up regular hours when he and they sit around the kitchen table doing their "homework." The rule is that he and the kids must be quiet for 45 minutes of every hour, but then can spend 15 minutes talking, during which time he can help them with their problems and explain what he is doing. They also share jokes and stories and tease and encourage each other during these 15-minute breaks.

You will need a place to study and store your school books and materials, a place that is comfortable and private (unless you're like Max), that has good lighting and a minimum of distracting clutter. It can be a card table in a corner of the bedroom or a mahogany desk in the den, but everyone else in the house has to recognize that it's yours and keep hands off.

There is no perfect way to study for everyone. You need to take account of your own preferences and timetable. Some people, if they have a lot of reading to do, stretch out on a bed to do it. Other people find that if they lie down they go to sleep, so they do their reading at a desk.

Make a study schedule for yourself and share it with the people with whom you live. Post it on the door or the refrigerator to generate support and sympathy. Here are a few general hints most students find helpful:

1. Always (or as much as possible) study in the same place. It seems to condition your brain in a positive way so that when you arrive at your study area, you concentrate more quickly. You are also less likely to lose things if you have one place to work.

2. Take regular breaks from reading. A walk to the kitchen sink for a glass of water will pep you up for another 10 pages. While you're on your break, talk out loud to yourself about what you've just read. If you can explain it to yourself you have a better chance of remembering it.

3. Study the hard stuff while you have the most energy. If math is tough for you, work on it first and then read your psychology assignment or *Moby Dick*. Avoid the temptation to do what you like first.

4. Don't forget the library. Not only is the library designed for study with good lighting, quiet areas and comfortable study furniture, but the librarian can help you find materials you need. In addition, in some courses the professor will have put some required reading books and journals on reserve, which means that you will have to spend time in the library reading them.

For a helpful list of tips for efficient study, see Appendix I.

Creating a Study Plan

You may be taking a typical three-hour English class, a standard requirement for any degree. Including reading and writing compositions, you will probably need to study five or six hours a week. Make a plan showing where and when you will study, including time at the library for research and time for typing weekly two- to three-page compositions required for the class.

Study Plan

class hours _____

study hours _____

library visits _____

study location _____

typewriter location _____

Study Skills

Study skills are those competencies that enable you to learn more easily, retain that learning, and demonstrate it through oral and written tests and compositions. They include:

reading efficiently;
remembering material;
understanding material;

taking notes;
using the library;
writing papers;
doing math problems;
preparing for tests; and
taking tests.

You're not born with study skills. You learn them. Most students, of all ages, come to school with weak study skills in some areas, but these weaker skills can be strengthened through books and programs, tutoring and practice. Many schools even offer a one-credit course in study skills, which might be worth your time and effort if you suspect you need help.

Although adults frequently worry that they may have forgotten how to study or will have a hard time competing with younger students, colleges' experience with adult students has demonstrated that adults are usually better students because they are motivated and have defined goals. Research tells us that returning adult students, on the average, maintain better grades than younger students.

While at first you may feel slightly ill at ease if there are a lot of younger students in your classes, you will find that your lifelong learning experiences and mature goals actually give you the edge. While younger students are partying on a Friday night, older students are often in the library. Older students seem better able to pace themselves, to study throughout the semester rather than cramming at the last minute.

Still, you probably haven't spent a lot of time reading or memorizing over the past few years. Some of your skills, such as in composition or math, may be a little rusty. But then younger students also have trouble with basic skills sometimes. That's why all colleges have basic skills centers (or tutoring centers or remedial skills centers — the names vary) where help is available to improve your reading speed and comprehension, composition skills, test-taking skills and basic math skills. Most centers offer assessment tests, sometimes called diagnostic tests, that give you an estimate of what your current skills levels are and how much help you may need. Experts can then assign you to specific learning programs

There is no perfect way to study for everyone. You need to take account of your own preferences and timetable.

designed to help you build your basic skills or can match you up with a tutor. Some basic skills programs are on computers and can be worked on at your own pace, concentrating exactly on those areas where you need the most help.

Basic skills services are usually free, and they work. Don't be shy about using them. They exist because there is a need for them, and they are designed to bring students up to speed as quickly as possible.

Trouble Shooting

No matter how well you have planned your return to school, glitches can occur. As a popular philosopher puts it, bad things can happen to good people. A college computer can fail so that you get to a class for which you have registered and your name isn't on the instructor's list. A course you really want may be cancelled for insufficient registration or changed to a time that is inconvenient. You can find yourself in a class that seems way above your head. The bookstore may have run out of copies of the chemistry text. You may get back your first history paper, on which you worked for hours and hours, and there's a huge "D" in the upper right hand corner. You don't like your advisor. You need a parking sticker and don't know where to go.

Well, the first thing to remember is, "Don't panic." The second is, "You aren't the first one who's ever had this problem. And there are always solutions." Think of yourself as a competent adult, with the ability to speak up for yourself. Also think of yourself as a consumer. You are paying a lot of money for an education. You have a right to make certain demands on the college.

You won't be the first or last one to challenge a *%$#*&! computer (or the human being who probably made the error), or to go to the registrar's office to change your schedule, or to make an appointment with an instructor to find out why he gave you a low grade, or to ask for help in understanding some knotty material. In fact, the more assertive you are about getting the information and help you need, the more people you will get to know

No matter how busy you are, try to make time to talk to your fellow students and professors, in and out of class. A college education can and should be far more than a series of classes taken, exams passed, credits accumulated and degrees awarded. Ideally, it is a series of learning experiences both in and out of the classroom that draw you into a learning society or learning culture.

on campus and the more respect you will have from others (and yourself). So ask questions. Track down the officials or faculty who can take positive action. Don't take no for an answer without finding out why. Look for alternatives. And above all, keep your sense of humor.

Not all of a College Education Occurs in the Classroom

OK. You have to race home after work to walk the dog. Then you hurry to the campus, arriving just in time for your class. After class you have to get back to relieve the babysitter, so you pass up the chance to ask the professor why he thinks Saul Bellow is a better writer than Stephen King, and you say no thanks to the couple sitting behind you who asked if you wanted to go out for a coffee. You may have blown your chance to enrich your education.

A college education can and should be far more than a series of classes taken, exams passed, credits accumulated and degrees awarded. A college education, ideally, is a series of learning experiences both in and out of the classroom that draw you into a learning society or learning culture. Going to college should give you access to a new friends, men and women who care about learning and who share it gladly. It should challenge your ideas, enlarge your horizons, make you think about people, art, politics, religion and the environment in new ways.

No matter how busy you are, try to make time to talk to your fellow students and professors, in and out of class; to read the college newspaper; and to attend special lectures or meetings on subjects that interest you. If there's an adult student organization on campus, join it. These extracurricular activities can open up whole new worlds for you and make the experience of going back to school more intellectually and personally stimulating than you ever dreamed.

A

Ten Standards for Quality Assurance in Assessing Learning for Credit

Academic Standards

1. Credit should be awarded only for learning and not for experience.

2. College credit should be awarded only for college-level learning.

3. Credit should be awarded only for learning that has a balance, appropriate to the subject, between theory and practical application.

4. The determination of competence levels and credit awards must be made by academic experts in the appropriate subject matter.

5. Credit should be appropriate to the academic context in which it is accepted.

Administrative Standards

6. Credit awards and their transcript entries should be monitored to avoid giving credit twice for the same learning.

7. Policies and procedures applied to assessment, including provision for appeal, should be fully disclosed and prominently available.

8. Fees charged for assessment should be based on the services performed in the process and not determined by the amount of credit awarded.

9. All personnel involved in the assessment of learning should receive adequate training for the functions they perform, and there should be provision for their continued professional development.

10. Assessment programs should be regularly monitored, reviewed, evaluated, and revised as needed to reflect changes in the needs being served and in the state of the assessment arts.

From Urban Whitaker, *Assessing Learning: Standards, Principles, and Procedures.* Philadelphia: CAEL, 1989.

A p p e n d i x

B

Useful Books for Career Planning

Bolles, Richard N. *The Three Boxes of Life: An Introduction to Life/Work Planning.* Berkeley, Calif.: Ten Speed Press, 1990.

Boles, Richard N. *What Color is Your Parachute? A Practical Manual for Job-Hunters and Career-Changers.* Berkeley, Calif.: Ten Speed Press, 1989.

> This deservedly popular book covers self-assessment, career planning and job hunting.

Careers Tomorrow: The Outlook for Work in a Changing World. Bethesda, Md.: World Future Society, 1983.

Holland, John, L. *Making Vocational Choices: A Theory of Vocational Personalities and Work Environments.* Englewood Cliffs, N.J.: Prentice-Hall, 1985.

Holland, John L. *The Self-Directed Search: A Guide to Educational and Vocational Planning.* Odessa, FL: Psychological Assessment Resources, 1985.

A short booklet with questions that help you explore your feelings and attitudes about different kinds of occupations. It is an excellent tool for helping people make basic career decisions.

Jackson, T. *Guerilla Tactics in the Job Market: A Practical Manual.* New York: Bantam Books, 1978.

Occupational Outlook Handbook. Washington, D.C.: U.S. Department of Labor, Bureau of Labor Statistics, 1990.

For each of the hundreds of occupations listed in this book, there is information on the nature of the work, working conditions, employment (numbers, types, locations), training needed, other qualifications, advancement, job outlook, earnings, and related occupations. (See your library or order from the Superintendent of Documents, U.S. Government Printing Office, Washington, D.C. 20402.)

Pearson, H. G. *Your Hidden Skills: Clues to Careers and Future Pursuits.* Wayland, Mass.: Mowry Press, 1981.

Pogrebin, L. C. *Getting Yours: How to Make the System Work for the Working Woman.* New York: McKay, 1975.

Rockcastle, Madeline T., ed. *Where to Start: An Annotated Career-Planning Bibliography.* Career Center, Cornell University; Peterson's Guides.

C

General Skills List

Management Skills	Communications Skills	Research Skills
Planning	Reasoning	Recognizing
Organizing	Organizing	problems
Scheduling	Defining	Interviewing
Assigning/	Writing	Developing
delegating	Listening	questions
Directing	Explaining	Synthesizing
Hiring	Interpreting ideas	Writing
Measuring	Reading	Diagnosing
production	Handle precision	Collecting data
Setting standards	work	Extrapolating
Work under stress	Work with	Reviewing
Work with people	committees	Work without
Travel frequently	Public speaking	direction

Management Skills	Communications Skills	Research Skills
Work as a team member	Correct English usage	Work very long hours
Personnel practices	Operate communication systems	Work on long term projects
Time management		Statistics
Negotiating strategies	Good sense of timing	Algebra
		Research design

Financial Skills	Manual Skills	Service Skills
Calculating	Operating	Counseling
Projecting	Monitoring	Guiding
Budgeting	Controlling	Leading
Recognize problems	Setting-up	Listening
Solve problems	Driving	Coordinating
Finger dexterity	Cutting	Work under stress
Orderly thinking	Work independently	Work on weekends
Accounting procedures	Knowledge of tools	Work night shifts
Data processing	Safety rules	Knowledge of a subject
Operate business machines	Basic mechanics	Human behavior principles
Financial concepts	Basic plumbing	Community resources
Investment principles	Electronic principles	Agencies' policies

Clerical Skills	Technical Skills	Public Relations Skills
Examining	Financial	Planning
Evaluating	Evaluating date	Conducting
Filing	Calculating	Maintaining favorable image
Developing methods	Adjusting controls	Informing the public
Improving	Aligning fixture	Consulting
Recording	Following specifications	Write news releases
Computating		

Clerical Skills	*Technical Skills*	*Public Relations Skills*
Recommending	Observing	Researching
Work as a team	indicators	Representing
member	Verifying	Work with people
Work in office	Drafting	Work under stress
Follow directions	Designing	Work very long
Do routine office	Work in an office/	hours
work	outdoors	Work odd hours
Basic clerical skills	Work in small	Negotiating
Bookkeeping	studios	principles
Data-entry	Odd hours	Media process
operations	Economics	Human relations
	Investigation	
	principles	
	Balancing	
	principles	

Agricultural Skills	*Selling Skills*	*Maintenance Skills*
Diagnosing	Contracting	Repairing
malfunctions	Persuading	equipment
Repairing engines	Reviewing products	Maintaining
Maintaining	Inspecting products	equipment
machinery	Determining value	Operating tools
Packing	Informing buyers	Dismantling
Replacing defective	Promoting sales	Removing parts
parts	Work outdoors/	Adjusting
Wood working	indoors	functional parts
Constructing	Work with people	Lubricating/
buildings	Work under stress	cleaning parts
Hitching	Work long hours	Purchasing/
Work outdoors	Knowledge of	ordering parts
Work in varied	products	Climbing
climate	Human relations	Work indoors/
Manual work	Financing	outdoors
Do heavy work	Budgeting	Lift heavy
Operating basic		equipment
machinery		

Agricultural Skills	Selling Skills	Maintenance Skills
Safety rules		Work as a team
Welding		member
Horticultural		Basic mechanics
procedures		Electrical principles
		Plumbing
		principles

D

Independent Learning Opportunities

Obtaining a college degree doesn't necessarily mean attending classes. There are a number of colleges and universities at which you may work toward an associate's, bachelor's or doctoral degree without attending a class. The following eight well-known "independent learning" options are among those that offer their programs to adults through various forms of distance learning. Each accepts out-of-state students and together they have graduated thousands of men and women whose degrees have led to personal and professional advancement. For further information call or write to:

American Open University of New York
Institute of Technology
Building 66, Office 227
Central Islip, NY 11722
(516) 348-3000

Center for Distance Learning
Empire State College
2 Union Avenue
Saratoga Springs, NY 12866
(518) 587-2100

Goddard College
Plainfield, VT 05667
(802) 454-8311

Mind Extension University
9697 East Mineral Avenue
Englewood, CO 80112-9920
(800) 777-MIND

Ohio University External Student Program
309 Tupper Hall
Athens, OH 45701
(800) 444-2420

Regents College of the University of the State of New York
Cultural Education Center
Albany, NY 12230
(518) 474-3703

Thomas A. Edison State College
101 West State Street
Trenton, NJ 08625
(609) 984-1100

The Union Institute
Undergraduate Studies
632 Vine Street, Suite 1010
Cincinnati, OH 45202
(513) 621-6444

E

Assessment Resources

Testing Programs

Advanced Placement Program (APP)

Tests in 13 academic subjects, usually taken by high school seniors for advanced placement in college courses, but may be accepted by some colleges as part of prior learning assessment. For further information write to:

Advanced Placement Program
Educational Testing Serice
Princeton, New Jersey 08541
(609) 771-7300

Proficiency Examination Program (ACT-PEP)

Over 40 tests covering the areas of nursing, business, arts and sciences, and education. For further information write to:

American College Testing Program
2255 N. Dubuque Road
Iowa City, IA 52243
(319) 337-1000

College Level Examination Program (CLEP)

The five general exams cover material taught in courses that most students take as requirements in the first two years of college: English composition, or English composition with essay; humanities; mathematics; natural sciences; and social sciences and history. The over 30 subject exams cover material taught in undergraduate courses in history, political science, psychology, economics, sociology, foreign language, composition and literature, science, mathematics and business. For further information write to:

CLEP
P.O. Box 661
Princeton, NJ 08541-6601
(215) 750-8420

Defense Activity for Non-Traditional Education Support (DANTES)

DANTES credit by examination tests are in subject areas somewhat different from CLEP subject tests but are constructed on similar principles, covering what would usually be learned in a semester-long college course. The DANTES program includes 49 tests in physical sciences, social sciences, business, applied technologies, foreign languages, humanities and mathematics. For further information write to:

DANTES Program Office
Educational Testing Service
Princeton, NJ 08541-0001
(215) 750-8328

Student Occupational Competency Achievement Tests (SOCAT)

The SOCAT tests are designed to measure proficiency in a broad range of occupational/vocational areas through written and performance tests. For further information contact:

National Occupational Competency Testing Institute
409 Bishop Hall
Ferris State University
Big Rapids, MI 49307
(616) 796-4695

Some Other Highly Respected Examination Programs

New York University Proficiency Testing in Foreign
    Languages
Foreign Language Program
NYU School of Continuing Education
2 University Place, Room 55
New York, NY 10003

Ohio University Examination Program
Lifelong Learning
309 Tupper Hall
Athens, OH 45701

Professional Secretaries International (PSI)
301 East Armour Blvd.
Kansas City, MO 64111-1299

Thomas A. Edison State College Examination Program
TECEP
Office of the Registrar
101 West State Street CN545
Trenton, NJ 08625

Licenses and Certificates in Professional Areas

Many colleges and universities use a student's possession of professional licenses and certificates as a basis for awarding credit for prior learning. Many of these professional licenses and certificates, in turn, are based on some combination of work experience, instruction, and examinations. Here is a partial listing of some widely recognized licenses and certificates.

Chartered Life Underwriter (CLU)
Chartered Property Casualty Underwriter (CPCU)
Certificate in Data Processing (CDP)
Certificate in Computer Programming (CCP)
Certified Professional Secretary (CPS)
Certified Public Accountant (CPA)
Chartered Financial Consultant (ChFC)
FAA Air Traffic Control Specialist
FAA Airline Transport Pilot
FAA Commercial Pilot Airplane License
FAA Commercial Pilot Rotocraft License
FAA Mechanic Certificate/Airframe and Power Plant Rating
FAA Multiengine Airplane
FAA Private Pilot Airplane License
FAA Private Pilot Rotocraft License
Registered Professional Reporter

A listing of other licenses, certificates and training programs that are creditworthy may be found in:

American Council on Education, *The National Guide to Educational Credit for Training Programs.* New York: Macmillan, 1986.

Evaluated Programs

These include:

Guide for the Program on Noncollegiate Sponsored Instruction (PONSI). Sponsored by the American Council on Education (ACE). PONSI evaluations have been done on several hundred corporate, union and government training programs.

A Guide to the Evaluation of Educational Experiences in the Armed Services. American Council on Education (ACE). Covers formal service school courses, correspondence courses with proctored end-of-the course examinations, Department of Defense (DOD) courses, Army military occupation specialties and Navy general rates and ratings.

F

Prior Learning Checklist

1. Previous colleges:

Name of College	*Major*	*Approximate Number of Credits*

2. Military service:

Service: _____ Year of discharge: _____

Training (see DD214 form): _____

_____

_____

3. Have you even taken any of the following tests?

CLEP _____ Other

GREs _____

DANTES _____ _____

4. Licenses held: Year received:

_____ _____

_____ _____

_____ _____

5. Apprentice training: Year completed:

_____ _____

_____ _____

_____ _____

6. Other training and nonaccredited courses:

Institution	Year(s)	Topic	Description
_____	_____	_____	_____
_____	_____	_____	_____
_____	_____	_____	_____

Use additional paper if necessary.

7. Job history:

Current Job Title	Years Held	Responsibilities
_____	_____	_____

Former Jobs	Years Held	Responsibilities
_____	_____	_____

Former Jobs   *Years Held*   *Responsibilities*

_____   _____   _____

Former Jobs   *Years Held*   *Responsibilities*

_____   _____   _____

Use additional paper if necessary.

8. Hobbies: _____

_____

_____

9. Foreign languages: _____

_____

10. Union involvement and experience:

_____

_____

_____

11. Organizational memberships:

Organization   *Offices Held*

_____   _____

_____   _____

_____   _____

12. Other areas of knowledge gained from reading, study, community involvement, etc.:

_____

_____

_____

_____

G

Learning Assessment Worksheet

Experience	Time Spent in Activity	Description of Duties, Tasks and Activities	Description of Learning Outcomes and Competencies	Documentation: Can You Suggest Ways an Evaluator Can Judge These?
Employment				
Education (noncredit courses and seminars)				
Volunteer Experience				
Recreation and Hobbies				

Experience	Time Spent in Activity	Description of Duties, Tasks and Activities	Description of Learning Outcomes and Competencies	Documentation: Can You Suggest Ways an Evaluator Can Judge These?
Military Experience				
Licenses, Awards, Publications				
Travel				
Professional Readings				

Experience	Time Spent in Activity	Description of Duties, Tasks and Activities	Description of Learning Outcomes and Competencies	Documentation: Can You Suggest Ways an Evaluator Can Judge These?
Other				
Other				
Other				
Other				

H

Documentation Worksheet

Sample

Learning Component	Type of Documentation	Date Sent For	Date Rec'd.	Present Location
Electronics	Navy discharge papers			Top drawer of desk
	Letter from boss at B&B Elec.	3/24	4/2	Under DOC in file
Management	Certificate of course at IBM			Under DOC in file
	Letter from IBM supervisor	3/24	4/16	Top drawer of desk

Learning Component	Type of Documentation	Date Sent For	Date Rec'd.	Present Location
	Transcript of Atwater College course in mgt.	3/27		
	Letter from ACME supervisor	3/24		
Accounting	CLEP test transcript	3/11	3/29	Under DOC in file
Painting	Small paintings			Living rm.
	Slides			Studio
	Letter from painting teacher	2/26	3/30	Under DOC in file
	Eval. of work by gallery owner	3/27		
Journalism	Eval. of work by Prof. James	4/17		Under DOC in file
	Copies of my news stories, reviews			Basement closet

Documentation Worksheet

Learning Component	Type of Documentation	Date Sent For	Date Rec'd.	Present Location

I

Study Tips

1. Make a schedule of your time and then stick to it.

2. Try to study in one particular place that is quiet and well lit (diffused lighting is best.)

3. Keep the top of your desk clear of distracting clutter (pictures, magazines, etc.).

4. Take short rests during long study sessions.

5. When you study, work to your maximum ability.

6. Start studying as soon as you sit down at your desk.

7. Always make a preliminary survey of your assignment before reading in detail.

8. As you study, evaluate what you are trying to learn. Ask yourself:

> *What* is it for?
> *How* does it work?
> *Why* is it expressed this way?
> *When* does it happen?

9. Remember that the type in which headings are printed is a clue to the importance of the material.

10. Study all graphs, drawings and tables; they are placed in the text for a purpose.

11. Be sure you know the meanings of all technical words in the text.

12. Always find the main thought in each paragraph.

13. Try to associate the ideas of the paragraphs and chapters of your assignment.

14. After studying the lesson carefully, summarize the content in your own words.

15. Use an abbreviated, outline form when taking notes.

16. Do not try to write down the exact words of the instructor.

17. Keep all notes on one subject together.

18. Devote one hour a week to weekly review in each subject.

19. If certain subject matter must be memorized, do not try to do it all at one time.

20. It is generally better to learn from, or memorize, the whole before the details.

21. Apply everything you learn as early and as often as possible.

22. During examination week, maintain regular habits and get your usual amount of sleep.

23. When taking a test, be sure to read all questions before answering any; outline the answers to essay questions before attempting to write them out.

24. When in class, pay attention to what is going on or you will miss important parts of the instructor's explanation of the lesson.

25. Do not miss class because you feel that you can make up the work. Try to get the phone number of a classmate — the buddy system is very helpful.

26. Do not hesitate to ask your instructor for help if you really need it.

J

Colleges & Universities

with Comprehensive Prior Learning Assessment Programs

In 1991, the Council for Adult and Experiential Learning (CAEL) surveyed all U.S. accredited institutions of higher education regarding their practices in the assessment of prior learning. The institutions listed in this appendix indicated that they provide opportunities for the assessment of prior learning for the award of college credit. Those institutions highlighted with an asterisk (*) responded that they offer at least three different options for comprehensive assessment.

ALABAMA

Alabama Aviation and
Technical College
Ozark   (205)774-5113

Auburn University
Auburn   (205)826-4000

Auburn University at Montgomery
Montgomery   (205)244-3000

Birmingham Southern College*
Birmingham   (205)226-4600

Brewer State Junior College
Fayette   (205)932-3221

Central Alabama
Community College
Alexander City   (205)234-6346

Community College of
the Air Force
Montgomery   (205)293-7064

Enterprise State Junior College
Enterprise   (205)347-2623

Faulkner University*
Montgomery   (205)272-5820

Gadsden State Community
College
Gadsden   (205)546-0484

George C. Wallace State
Community College—Dothan
Dothan   (205)983-3521

Jacksonville State University
Jacksonville   (205)782-5781

Jefferson State Community
College
Birmingham   (205)853-1200

John C. Calhoun State
Community College
Decatur   (205)353-3102

John M. Patterson State
Technical College
Montgomery   (205)288-1080

Judson College*
Marion   (205)683-6161

Livingston University
Livingston   (205)652-9661

Lurleen B. Wallace State
Junior College
Andalusia   (205)222-6591

Mobile College*
Mobile   (205)675-5990

Samford University*
Birmingham   (205)870-2011

Snead State Junior College
Boaz   (205)593-5120

Stillman College*
Tuscaloosa   (205)349-4240

Troy State University*
Troy   (205)566-8112

Troy State University at Dothan
Dothan   (205)983-6556

Troy State University in
Montgomery*
Montgomery   (205)834-1400

University of Alabama in
Huntsville
Huntsville   (205)895-6120

University of Montevallo*
Montevallo   (205)665-6000

University of South Alabama
Mobile   (205)460-6101

Walker College
Jasper   (205)387-0511

Wallace State Community
College—Hanceville
Hanceville   (205)352-6403

*Institution indicates *comprehensive* prior learning assessment available.

ALASKA

Sheldon Jackson College*
Sitka   (907)747-5220

University of Alaska Anchorage*
Anchorage   (907)786-1800

University of Alaska Fairbanks*
Fairbanks   (907)474-7112

ARIZONA

Arizona State University
Tempe   (602)965-9011

Central Arizona College*
Coolidge, AZ 85228 (602)426-4444

Eastern Arizona College
Thatcher   (602)428-1133

Gateway Community College*
Phoenix   (602)275-8500

Glendale Community College*
Glendale   (818)240-1000

Mesa Community College*
Mesa   (602)461-7000

Mohave Community College
Kingman   (602)757-4331

Northern Arizona University*
Flagstaff   (602)523-9011

Northland Pioneer College*
Holbrook   (602)524-6111

Pima County Community College
  District*
Tucson   (602)884-6666

Prescott College
Prescott   (602)778-2090

Rio Salado College*
Phoenix   (602)223-4000

University Of Phoenix*
Phoenix   (602)966-9577

ARKANSAS

East Arkansas Community College*
Forrest City   (501)633-4480

Garland County Community
  College*
Hot Springs   (501)767-9371

Harding University Main Campus*
Searcy   (501)279-4000

Mississippi County Community
  College*
Blytheville   (501)762-1020

North Arkansas Community
  College
Harrison   (501)743-3000

Phillips County Community College
Helena   (501)338-6474

Southern Arkansas University*
Magnolia   (501)235-4000

Southern Arkansas University Tech*
Camden   (501)574-4500

University Of Arkansas At
  Pine Bluff
Pine Bluff   (501)541-6500

University Of Central Arkansas
Conway   (501)329-2931

University Of The Ozarks
Clarksville   (501)754-3839

Westark Community College
Fort Smith   (501)785-7000

Williams Baptist College
Walnut Ridge   (501)886-6741

*Institution indicates *comprehensive* prior learning assessment available.

CALIFORNIA

Bakersfield College
Bakersfield   (805)395-4011

Barstow College*
Barstow   (619)252-2411

Biola University
La Mirada   (213)944-0351

Brooks Institute*
Santa Barbara   (805)966-3888

California Baptist College*
Riverside   (714)689-5771

California College Of Arts And
  Crafts
Oakland   (415)653-8118

California Polytechnic State
  University — San Luis Obispo
San Luis Obispo   (805)756-0111

California State Polytechnic
  University — Pomona*
Pomona   (714)869-2000

California State University —
  Bakersfield*
Bakersfield   (805)664-2011

California State University —
  Fullerton
Fullerton   (714)773-2011

California State University —
  Hayward
Hayward   (415)881-3000

California State University —
  Long Beach
Long Beach   (213)985-4111

Cerro Coso Community College
Ridgecrest   (619)375-5001

Chabot College
Hayward   (415)786-6600

Christ College Irvine
Irvine   (714)854-8002

Claremont McKenna College
Claremont   (714)621-8111

Coleman College
La Mesa   (619)465-3990

College Of Notre Dame
Belmont   (415)593-1601

College Of San Mateo
San Mateo   (415)574-6161

College Of The Canyons
Santa Clarita   (805)259-7800

College Of The Sequoias
Visalia   (209)733-2050

College Of The Siskiyous
Weed   (916)938-4461

Cosumnes River College
Sacramento   (916)688-7451

Crafton Hills College
Yucaipa   (714)794-2161

De Anza College
Cupertino   (408)864-8567

Don Bosco Technical Institute*
Rosemead   (818)280-0451

East Los Angeles College
Monterey Park   (213)265-8650

Fashion Institute Of Design And
  Merchandising
Los Angeles   (213)624-1200

Feather River Community College
  District*
Quincy   (916)283-0202

Fresno City College*
Fresno   (209)442-4600

Gavilan College*
Gilroy   (408)847-1400

*Institution indicates *comprehensive* prior learning assessment available.

Golden Gate University
San Francisco   (415)442-7000

Harvey Mudd College
Claremont   (714)621-8000

Holy Names College
Oakland   (415)436-1000

ITT Technical Institute
Sacramento   (208)344-8376

Kings River Community College
Reedley   (209)638-3641

Los Angeles City College
Los Angeles   (213)669-4000

Los Angeles Harbor College
Wilmington   (213)518-1000

Los Angeles Mission College
San Fernando   (818)365-8271

Los Angeles Pierce College
Woodland Hills   (818)347-0551

Los Angeles Valley College
Van Nuys   (818)781-1200

Loyola Marymount University
Los Angeles   (213)338-2700

Menlo College
Menlo Park   (415)323-6141

Mira Costa College
Oceanside   (619)757-2121

Modesto Junior College
Modesto   (209)575-6498

Monterey Institute Of
  International Studies*
Monterey   (408)647-4100

Mount Saint Mary's College*
Los Angeles   (213)476-2237

Napa Valley College
Napa   (707)253-3095

National University
San Diego   (619)563-7100

New College Of California*
San Francisco   (415)626-1694

Northrop University
Los Angeles   (213)337-4413

Orange Coast College*
Costa Mesa   (714)432-0202

Pacific Christian College*
Fullerton   (714)879-3901

Pacific Oaks College*
Pasadena   (818)397-1300

Palomar College
San Marcos   (619)744-1150

Pitzer College
Claremont   (714)621-8000

Point Loma Nazarene College
San Diego   (619)221-2200

Porterville College
Porterville   (209)781-3130

Rio Hondo College
Whittier   (213)692-0921

SAMRA University Of Oriental
  Medicine*
Los Angeles   (213)487-2672

Saddleback College*
Mission Viejo   (714)582-4500

San Diego Community College
San Diego   (619)584-6500

San Diego Mesa College
San Diego   (619)560-2600

San Diego Miramar College
San Diego   (619)693-6800

San Diego State University
San Diego   (619)594-5200

San Francisco Art Institute
San Francisco   (415)771-7020

San Francisco Community College
  District
San Francisco   (415)239-3000

*Institution indicates *comprehensive* prior learning assessment available.

Santa Barbara City College
Santa Barbara   (805)965-0581

Santa Clara University
Santa Clara   (408)554-4764

Santa Monica College
Santa Monica   (213)450-5150

Santa Rosa Junior College
Santa Rosa   (707)527-4011

Scripps College
Claremont   (714)621-8000

Simpson College
Redding   (916)222-6360

Skyline College
San Bruno   (415)355-7000

Southern California College
Costa Mesa   (714)556-3610

Stanford University
Stanford   (415)723-2300

The Master's College
Newhall   (805)259-3540

University Of California — Davis
Davis   (916)752-1011

University Of California —
  Los Angeles
Los Angeles   (213)825-4321

University Of Judaism
Los Angeles   (213)476-9777

University Of La Verne*
La Verne   (714)593-3511

University Of Redlands*
Redlands   (714)793-2121

University Of San Diego
San Diego   (619)260-4600

University Of San Francisco*
San Francisco   (415)666-6886

University Of Southern California
Los Angeles   (213)743-2311

University Of The Pacific*
Stockton   (209)946-2011

University Of West Los Angeles
Culver City   (213)313-1011

West Coast University Main
  Campus
Los Angeles   (213)487-4433

West Hills Community College
Coalinga   (209)935-0801

West Valley College
Saratoga   (408)867-2200

Whittier College
Whittier   (213)693-0771

Woodbury University
Los Angeles   (818)767-0888

COLORADO

Adams State College
Alamosa   (719)589-7121

Aims Community College
Greeley   (303)330-8008

Arapahoe Community College*
Littleton   (303)794-1550

Beth-El College Of Nursing
Colorado Springs   (719)475-5170

Colorado College
Colorado Springs   (719)389-6000

Colorado Northwestern
  Community College*
Rangely   (303)675-2261

Colorado State University
Fort Collins   (303)491-1101

Community College Of Denver*
Denver   (303)556-2481

Denver Automotive And Diesel
  College
Denver   (303)722-5724

*Institution indicates *comprehensive* prior learning assessment available.

Denver Conservative Baptist
  Seminary
Denver   (303)761-2482

Fort Lewis College
Durango   (303)247-7010

Front Range Community College*
Westminster   (303)466-8811

Morgan Community College*
Fort Morgan   (303)867-3081

Northeastern Junior College*
Sterling   (303)522-6600

Otero Junior College*
La Junta   (303)384-8721

Pikes Peak Community College*
Colorado Springs (719)576-7711

Pueblo Community College*
Pueblo   (719)549-3200

Red Rocks Community College*
Lakewood   (303)988-6160

Regis College*
Denver   (303)458-4100

Rocky Mountain College Of Art
  And Desgn*
Denver   (303)753-6046

The Naropa Institute
Boulder   (303)444-0202

University Of Colorado Health
  Sciences Center
Denver   (303)399-1211

University Of Colorado, Boulder
Boulder   (303)492-0111

University Of Denver
Denver   (303)871-2000

Western State College
Gunnison   (303)943-0120

CONNECTICUT

Albertus Magnus College*
New Haven   (203)773-8550

Briarwood College*
Southington   (203)628-4751

Charter Oak College*
Farmington   (203)677-0076

Connecticut College
New London   (203)447-1911

Eastern Connecticut State
  University*
Willimantic   (203)456-2231

Fairfield University*
Fairfield   (203)254-4000

Hartford Seminary
Hartford   (203)232-4451

Hartford State Technical College
Hartford   (203)527-4111

Housatonic Community College*
Bridgeport   (203)579-6400

Mattatuck Community College*
Waterbury   (203)575-8044

Middlesex Community College*
Middletown   (203)344-3011

Mohegan Community College*
Norwich   (203)886-1931

Norwalk Community College*
Norwalk   (203)853-2040

Sacred Heart University*
Fairfield   (203)371-7999

Saint Joseph College*
West Hartford   (203)232-4571

Teikyo Post University*
Waterbury   (203)755-0121

*Institution indicates *comprehensive* prior learning assessment available.

United States Coast Guard
Academy
New London   (203)444-8444

University Of Bridgeport*
Bridgeport   (203)576-4000

University Of Hartford*
West Hartford   (203)243-4100

DELAWARE

Goldey Beacom College
Wilmington   (302)998-8814

Wesley College*
Dover   (302)736-2300

DISTRICT OF COLUMBIA

Catholic University Of America
Washington   (202)319-5000

Corcoran School Of Art
Washington   (202)628-9484

George Washington University
Washington   (202)994-1000

Mount Vernon College
Washington   (202)331-3444

Southeastern University*
Washington   (202)488-8162

The American University*
Washington   (202)885-1000

FLORIDA

Barry University*
Miami Shores   (305)758-3392

Bethune Cookman College
Daytona Beach   (904)255-1401

Brevard Community College*
Cocoa   (407)632-1111

Central Florida Community College
Ocala   (904)237-2111

Chipola Junior College
Marianna   (904)526-2761

Daytona Beach Community
College*
Daytona Beach   (904)255-8131

Edison Community College*
Fort Myers   (813)489-9300

Embry-Riddle Aeronautical
University*
Daytona Beach   (904)239-6000

Flagler College
Saint Augustine   (904)829-6481

Florida Agricultural And
Mechanical University*
Tallahassee   (904)599-3000

Florida Atlantic University
Boca Raton   (407)367-3000

Florida Baptist Theological College
Graceville   (904)263-3261

Florida College
Temple Terrace   (813)988-5131

Florida Community College At
Jacksonville
Jacksonville   (904)632-3000

Florida Institute Of Technology
Melbourne   (407)768-8000

Florida International University*
Miami   (305)348-2000

Florida Keys Community College
Key West   (305)296-9081

Florida State University
Tallahassee   (904)644-2525

*Institution indicates *comprehensive* prior learning assessment available.

Hillsborough Community College
Tampa   (813)253-7000

Indian River Community College
Fort Pierce   (407)468-4700

Liberty Bible College*
Pensacola   (904)453-3451

Miami Christian College*
Miami   (305)685-7431

National Education Center — Tampa
  Technical Institute Campus
Tampa   (813)238-0455

North Florida Junior College
Madison   (904)973-2288

Nova University*
Fort Lauderdale   (305)475-7300

Okaloosa-Walton Community
  College
Niceville   (904)678-5111

Orlando College*
Orlando   (407)628-5870

Palm Beach Atlantic College*
West Palm Beach   (407)650-7700

Palm Beach Community College*
Lake Worth   (407)439-8000

Pensacola Junior College*
Pensacola   (904)484-1000

Polk Community College*
Winter Haven   (813)297-1000

Ringling School Of Art And Design
Sarasota   (813)351-4614

Rollins College
Winter Park   (407)646-2000

Seminole Community College
Sanford   (407)323-1450

South Florida Community College*
Avon Park   (813)453-6661

Southeastern College Of The
  Assemblies Of God*
Lakeland   (813)665-4404

St. Leo College
Saint Leo   (904)588-8200

St. Petersburg Junior College*
Saint Petersburg   (813)341-3600

Stetson University
Deland   (904)822-7000

Tampa College*
Tampa   (813)879-6000

University Of Central Florida
Orlando   (407)275-2000

University Of Florida
Gainesville   (904)392-3261

University Of Miami
Coral Gables   (305)284-2211

University Of South Florida
Tampa   (813)974-2235

University Of Tampa*
Tampa   (813)253-3333

University Of West Florida
Pensacola   (904)474-2000

Warner Southern College*
Lake Wales   (813)638-1426

Webber College*
Babson Park   (813)638-1431

GEORGIA

Agnes Scott College
Decatur   (404)371-6000

Andrew College
Cuthbert   (912)732-2171

Atlanta Christian College
East Point   (404)761-8861

*Institution indicates *comprehensive* prior learning assessment available.

Augusta College
Augusta   (404)737-1400

Augusta Technical Institute*
Augusta   (404)796-6900

Bainbridge College
Bainbridge   (912)248-2500

Berry College
Mount Berry   (404)232-5374

Brenau College*
Gainesville   (404)534-6299

Brunswick College
Brunswick   (912)264-7235

Chattahooche Technical Institute
Marietta   (404)528-4500

Dalton College
Dalton   (404)272-4436

Darton College
Albany   (912)888-8740

DeKalb Technical Institute*
Clarkston   (404)297-9522

DeVry Institute Of Technology*
Atlanta   (312)929-8500

Emmanuel College
Franklin Springs   (404)245-7226

Emmanuel College School Of
   Christian Ministries
Franklin Springs   (404)245-7226

Fort Valley State College*
Fort Valley   (912)825-6315

Georgia College
Milledgeville   (912)453-5350

Georgia Institute Of Technology
Atlanta   (404)894-2000

Georgia Military College*
Milledgeville   (912)453-3481

Georgia Southern University
Statesboro   (912)681-5611

Georgia State University*
Atlanta   (404)651-2000

Kennesaw State College
Marietta   (404)423-6000

Life College
Marietta   (404)424-0554

Macon College
Macon   (912)471-2700

Meadows College Of Business
Columbus   (404)327-7668

Medical College Of Georgia
Augusta   (404)721-0211

Oglethorpe University
Atlanta   (404)261-1441

Paine College
Augusta   (404)722-4471

Piedmont College
Demorest   (404)778-8009

Savannah Area Vocational—
   Technical School*
Savannah   (912)352-1464

Shorter College*
Rome   (501)374-6305

South College
Savannah   (912)651-8100

South Georgia College
Douglas   (912)383-4231

Spelman College
Atlanta   (404)681-3643

Toccoa Falls College
Toccoa Falls   (404)886-6831

University Of Georgia
Athens   (404)542-3030

Valdosta State College
Valdosta   (912)333-5952

Waycross College
Waycross   (912)285-6130

*Institution indicates *comprehensive* prior learning assessment available.

Wesleyan College*
Macon   (912)477-1110

West Georgia College
Carrollton   (404)836-6500

GUAM

University Of Guam
Mangilao   (671)734-2177

HAWAII

Hawaii Loa College*
Kaneohe   (808)235-3641

University Of Hawaii West Oahu
Aiea   (808)456-5921

IDAHO

Boise State University*
Boise   (208)385-1011

College Of Idaho
Caldwell   (208)459-5500

Idaho State University*
Pocatello   (208)236-0211

Lewis-Clark State College*
Lewiston   (208)799-5272

Northwest Nazarene College
Nampa   (208)467-8011

University Of Idaho*
Moscow   (208)885-6111

ILLINOIS

American Academy Of Art
Chicago   (312)939-3883

Aurora University*
Aurora   (708)892-6431

Belleville Area College
Belleville   (618)235-2700

Black Hawk College District Office
Moline   (309)796-1311

Black Hawk College East Campus*
Kewanee   (309)852-5671

Blackburn College
Carlinville   (217)854-3231

Board Of Governors Of State
  Colleges And Universities*
Springfield   (217)782-6392

Bradley University
Peoria   (309)676-7611

Chicago State University
Chicago   (312)995-2400

City Colleges Of Chicago
  Malcolm X College
Chicago   (312)942-3000

City Colleges of Chicago
Chicago   (312)641-0808

College Of Du Page
Glen Ellyn   (708)858-2800

College Of Lake County
Grayslake   (708)223-6601

College Of Saint Francis*
Joliet   (815)740-3360

Columbia College*
Chicago   (312)663-1600

Concordia University*
River Forest   (708)771-8300

De Paul University*
Chicago   (312)341-8000

DeVry Institute Of Technology
Chicago   (312)929-8500

Eastern Illinois University*
Charleston   (217)581-5000

*Institution indicates *comprehensive* prior learning assessment available.

Elgin Community College*
Elgin   (708)697-1000

Elmhurst College*
Elmhurst   (708)279-4100

Greenville College*
Greenville   (618)664-1840

Highland Community College*
Freeport   (815)235-6121

Illinois Central College
East Peoria   (309)694-5011

Illinois College
Jacksonville   (217)245-3000

International Academy Of
  Merchandising And Design*
Chicago   (312)828-0202

John Wood Community College*
Quincy   (217)224-6500

Joliet Junior College
Joliet   (815)729-9020

Kaes College
Chicago   (312)725-1925

Kaskaskia College*
Centralia   (618)532-1981

Knox College
Galesburg   (309)343-0112

Lake Forest College
Lake Forest   (708)234-3100

Lake Land College*
Mattoon   (217)235-3131

Lakeview College Of Nursing
Danville   (217)443-5238

Lewis University*
Romeoville   (815)838-0500

Lincoln Land Community College*
Springfield   (217)786-2200

Loyola University Of Chicago
Chicago   (312)915-6000

MacMurray College
Jacksonville   (217)245-6151

McHenry County College
Crystal Lake   (815)455-3700

Millikin University
Decatur   (217)424-6211

Monmouth College
Monmouth   (309)457-2311

Montay College
Chicago   (312)539-1919

Moraine Valley Community College*
Palos Hills   (312)974-4300

Morton College*
Cicero   (708)656-8000

Mundelein College
Chicago   (312)262-8100

National-Louis University*
Evanston   (708)475-1100

Northeastern Illinois University*
Chicago   (312)583-4050

Northern Illinois University
De Kalb   (815)753-1000

Northwestern University
Evanston   (708)491-3741

Parkland College*
Champaign   (217)351-2200

Prairie State College
Chicago Heights   (708)756-3110

Principia College*
Elsah   (618)374-2131

Quincy College*
Quincy   (217)222-8020

Rock Valley College
Rockford   (815)654-4250

Rockford College
Rockford   (815)226-4000

*Institution indicates *comprehensive* prior learning assessment available.

Roosevelt University*
Chicago   (312)341-3500

Rosary College
River Forest   (708)366-2490

Saint Augustine College
Chicago   (312)878-8756

Sangamon State University*
Springfield   (217)786-6600

South Suburban College Of Cook
   County
South Holland   (708)596-2000

Southeastern Illinois College
Harrisburg   (618)252-6376

Southern Illinois University At
   Carbondale*
Carbondale   (618)453-2121

Southern Illinois University At
   Edwardsville
Edwardsville   (618)692-2000

St. Joseph College Of Nursing*
Joliet   (815)725-7133

Trinity Christian College
Palos Heights   (708)597-3000

Trinity College*
Deerfield   (203)297-2000
University Of Illinois At
   Urbana-Champaign
Urbana   (217)333-1000

Wheaton College
Wheaton   (708)260-5000

William Rainey Harper College
Palatine   (708)397-3000

INDIANA

Anderson University
Anderson   (317)649-9071

Bethel College*
Mishawaka   (219)259-8511

Earlham College
Richmond   (317)983-1200

Franklin College Of Indiana
Franklin   (317)736-8441

Goshen College*
Goshen   (219)535-7000

Holy Cross College
Notre Dame   (219)233-6813

Huntington College
Huntington   (219)356-6000

Indiana University At Bloomington*
Bloomington   (812)332-0211

Indiana University Northwest*
Gary   (219)980-6500

Indiana University Southeast*
New Albany   (812)941-2000

Indiana University — Purdue
   University At Indianapolis*
Indianapolis   (317)274-5555

Indiana Vocational Technical
   Central Office*
Indianapolis   (317)921-4882

Indiana Vocational Technical
   College — Eastcentral*
Muncie   (317)289-2291

Indiana Vocational Technical
   College — Northcentral*
South Bend   (219)289-7001

Indiana Vocational Technical
   College — Northeast*
Fort Wayne   (219)482-9171

Indiana Vocational Technical
   College — Southcentral*
Sellersburg   (812)246-3301

Indiana Vocational Technical
   College — Southeast
Madison   (812)265-2580

*Institution indicates *comprehensive* prior learning assessment available.

Indiana Vocational Technical
College — Southwest*
Evansville   (812)426-2865

Indiana Wesleyan University*
Marion   (317)674-6901

International Business College
Fort Wayne   (219)432-8702

Manchester College
North Manchester   (219)982-5000

Marian College
Indianapolis   (317)929-0123

Martin Center College*
Indianapolis   (317)543-3235

Oakland City College*
Oakland City   (812)749-4781

Purdue University Calumet*
Hammond   (219)989-2993

Purdue University Main Campus
West Lafayette   (317)494-4600

Purdue University North Central
Campus
Westville   (219)785-5200

Saint Francis College*
Fort Wayne   (219)432-3551

Saint Joseph's College
Rensselaer   (219)866-6000

Saint Mary's College
Notre Dame   (219)284-4000

Saint Mary-Of-The-Woods College*
Saint Mary-Of-The-Woods
                      (812)535-5151

Saint Meinrad College
Saint Meinrad   (812)357-6611

Summit Christian College
Fort Wayne   (219)456-2111

Taylor University
Upland   (317)998-2751

University Of Evansville*
Evansville   (812)477-6241

University Of Notre Dame
Notre Dame   (219)239-5000

University Of Southern Indiana
Evansville   (812)464-8600

Valparaiso University
Valparaiso   (219)464-5000

Vincennes University*
Vincennes   (812)882-3350

Wabash College
Crawfordsville   (317)362-1400

IOWA

Briar Cliff College*
Sioux City   (712)279-5321

Buena Vista College*
Storm Lake   (712)749-2351

Central University Of Iowa
Pella   (515)628-9000

Clarke College*
Dubuque   (319)588-6300

Coe College
Cedar Rapids   (319)399-8000

Cornell College
Mount Vernon   (319)895-4000

Des Moines Area Community
College*
Ankeny   (515)964-6200

Drake University*
Des Moines   (515)271-2011

Eastern Iowa Community College
Davenport   (319)322-5015

Faith Baptist Bible College And
Seminary
Ankeny   (515)964-0601

*Institution indicates *comprehensive* prior learning assessment available.

Graceland College*
Lamoni   (515)784-5000

Grinnell College
Grinnell   (515)269-4000

Indian Hills Community College
Ottumwa   (515)683-5111

Iowa Central Community College
Fort Dodge   (515)576-7201

Iowa Lakes Community College*
Estherville   (712)362-2601

Iowa State University
Ames   (515)294-4111

Iowa Wesleyan College*
Mount Pleasant   (319)385-8021

Iowa Western Community College*
Council Bluffs   (712)325-3200

Loras College*
Dubuque   (319)588-7100

Marycrest College*
Davenport   (319)326-9512

Mount Mercy College*
Cedar Rapids   (319)363-8213

Mount Saint Clare College
Clinton   (319)242-4023

Muscatine Community College*
Muscatine   (319)263-8250

North Iowa Area Community
   College*
Mason City   (515)423-1264

Northwestern College
Orange City   (712)737-4821

Simpson College*
Indianola   (916)222-6360

Southeastern Community College
W Burlington   (919)642-7141

Southwestern Community College
Creston   (515)782-7081

St. Ambrose University*
Davenport   (319)383-8800

University Of Iowa
Iowa City   (319)335-3500

University Of Northern Iowa*
Cedar Falls   (319)273-2311

Upper Iowa University*
Fayette   (319)425-5200

Waldorf College*
Forest City   (515)582-2450

Wartburg Theological Seminary
Dubuque   (319)589-0200

Western Iowa Tech Community
   College
Sioux City   (712)274-6400

Westmar College*
Le Mars   (712)546-7081

William Penn College
Oskaloosa   (515)673-1001

KANSAS

Allen County Community College
Iola   (316)365-5116

Baker University*
Baldwin City   (913)594-6451

Barclay College*
Haviland   (316)862-5252

Barton County Community College
Great Bend   (316)792-2701

Benedictine College
Atchison   (913)367-5340

Bethel College
North Newton   (219)259-8511

Butler County Community College
El Dorado   (316)321-5083

*Institution indicates *comprehensive* prior learning assessment available.

Dodge City Community College
Dodge City   (316)225-1321

Donnelly College*
Kansas City   (913)621-6070

Emporia State University
Emporia   (316)343-1200

Fort Hays State University
Hays   (913)628-4000

Friends University*
Wichita   (316)261-5800

Hesston College
Hesston   (316)327-4221

Highland Community College
Highland   (815)235-6121

Hutchinson Community College
Hutchinson   (316)665-3500

Independence Community College
Independence   (316)331-4100

Johnson County Community
  College*
Overland Park   (913)469-8500

Kansas City Kansas Community
  College*
Kansas City   (913)334-1100

Kansas Newman College*
Wichita   (316)942-4291

Kansas State University*
Manhattan   (913)532-6011

MidAmerica Nazarene College*
Olathe   (913)782-3750

Ottawa University*
Ottawa   (913)242-5200

Pittsburg State University
Pittsburg   (316)231-7000

Pratt Community College
Pratt   (316)672-5641

Saint Mary College*
Leavenworth   (913)682-5151

Saint Mary Of The Plains College*
Dodge City   (316)225-4171

Southwestern College*
Winfield   (619)421-6700

Tabor College
Hillsboro   (316)947-3121

The Wichita State University*
Wichita   (316)689-3456

University Of Kansas Main Campus
Lawrence   (913)864-2700

Washburn University Of Topeka
Topeka   (913)295-6300

KENTUCKY

Alice Lloyd College
Pippa Passes   (606)368-2101

Asbury College
Wilmore   (606)858-3511

Bellarmine College*
Louisville   (502)452-8211

Berea College
Berea   (606)986-9341

Brescia College*
Owensboro   (502)685-3131

Campbellsville College*
Campbellsville   (502)465-8158

Centre College
Danville   (606)236-5211

Eastern Kentucky University
Richmond   (606)622-2101

Elizabethtown Community College
Elizabethtown   (502)769-2371

Franklin College
Paducah   (502)443-8478

Georgetown College
Georgetown   (502)863-8011

*Institution indicates *comprehensive* prior learning assessment available.

Hazard Community College
Hazard   (606)436-5721

Hopkinsville Community College
Hopkinsville   (502)886-3921

Kentucky State University*
Frankfort   (502)227-6000

Kentucky Wesleyan College*
Owensboro   (502)926-3111

Lees College*
Jackson   (606)666-7521

Maysville Community College*
Maysville   (606)759-7141

Midway College
Midway   (606)846-4421

Morehead State University
Morehead   (606)783-2221

Murray State University*
Murray   (502)762-3011

Northern Kentucky University*
Highland Heights   (606)572-5100

Owensboro Community College
Owensboro   (502)686-4400

Pikeville College*
Pikeville   (606)432-9200

Somerset Community College
Somerset   (606)679-8501

Southeast Community College
Cumberland   (402)471-3303

Spalding University*
Louisville   (502)585-9911

St. Catharine College
Saint Catharine   (606)336-9303

Thomas More College*
Fort Mitchell   (606)341-5800

Transylvania University
Lexington   (606)233-8300

Union College*
Barbourville   (606)546-4151

University Of Kentucky*
Lexington   (606)257-9000

Western Kentucky University
Bowling Green   (502)745-0111

LOUISIANA

Centenary College Of Louisiana
Shreveport   (318)869-5011

Dillard University
New Orleans   (504)283-8822

Louisiana College
Pineville   (318)487-7011

Louisiana State University
  Agricultural/Mechanical College
Baton Rouge   (504)388-3202

Louisiana State University At
  Alexandria
Alexandria   (318)445-3672

Louisiana State University At
  Eunice
Eunice   (318)457-7311

Louisiana Tech University
Ruston   (318)257-0211

McNeese State University*
Lake Charles   (318)475-5000

Our Lady Of Holy Cross College*
New Orleans   (504)394-7744

Southeastern Louisiana University
Hammond   (504)549-2000

Southern University At New
  Orleans
New Orleans   (504)286-5000

St. Joseph Seminary College*
Saint Benedict   (504)892-1800

*Institution indicates *comprehensive* prior learning assessment available.

University Of New Orleans
New Orleans   (504)286-6000

Xavier University Of Louisiana
New Orleans   (504)486-7411

MAINE

Andover College*
Portland   (207)774-6126

Bowdoin College
Brunswick   (207)725-3000

Central Maine Medical Center
School Of Nursing
Lewiston   (207)795-2840

Central Maine Technical College*
Auburn   (207)784-2385

Maine Maritime Academy*
Castine   (207)326-4311

Saint Joseph's College*
Windham   (219)866-6000

Unity College
Unity   (207)948-3131

University Of Maine*
Orono   (207)581-1110

University Of Maine At Fort Kent*
Fort Kent   (207)834-3162

University Of Maine At Presque Isle
Presque Isle   (207)764-0311

University Of New England*
Biddeford   (207)283-0171

MARYLAND

Allegany Community College
Cumberland   (301)724-7700

Bowie State University*
Bowie   (301)464-3000

Catonsville Community College*
Catonsville   (301)455-6050

Chesapeake College*
Wye Mills   (301)822-5400

Columbia Union College*
Takoma Park   (301)270-9200

Coppin State College
Baltimore   (301)383-4500

Dundalk Community College*
Baltimore   (301)282-6700

Frederick Community College
Frederick   (301)694-5240

Garrett Community College*
McHenry   (301)387-6666

Goucher College*
Towson   (301)337-6000

Hagerstown Business College
Hagerstown   (301)739-2670

Hagerstown Junior College
Hagerstown   (301)790-2800

Howard Community College*
Columbia   (301)992-4800

Johns Hopkins University
Baltimore   (301)338-8000

Loyola College in Maryland
Baltimore   (301)323-1010

Prince George's Community
College*
Largo   (301)336-6000

Towson State University*
Baltimore   (301)321-2000

Traditional Acupuncture Institute
Columbia   (301)596-6006

United States Naval Academy
Annapolis   (301)267-6100

University Of Baltimore
Baltimore   (301)625-3000

*Institution indicates *comprehensive* prior learning assessment available.

University Of Maryland Baltimore
County
Catonsville   (301)455-1000

University Of Maryland University
College*
College Park   (301)985-7000

Western Maryland College*
Westminster   (301)848-7000

MASSACHUSETTS

Anna Maria College*
Paxton   (508)757-4586

Assumption College
Worcester   (508)752-5615

Bentley College
Waltham   (617)891-2000

Berkshire Community College*
Pittsfield   (413)499-4660

Boston College
Chestnut Hill   (617)552-8000

Boston Conservatory*
Boston   (617)536-6340

Boston University
Boston   (617)353-2000

Bradford College
Bradford   (508)372-7161

Brandeis University
Waltham   (617)736-2000

Bristol Community College*
Fall River   (617)678-2811

Cape Cod Community College*
West Barnstable   (508)362-2131

College Of Our Lady Of The Elms*
Chicopee   (413)594-2761

College Of The Holy Cross
Worcester   (508)793-2011

Curry College*
Milton   (617)333-0500

Dean Junior College
Franklin   (508)528-9100

Emerson College
Boston   (617)578-8500

Emmanuel College*
Boston   (404)245-7226

Endicott College*
Beverly   (508)927-0585

Gordon College
Wenham   (404)358-5000

Greenfield Community College*
Greenfield   (413)774-3131

Harvard University
Cambridge   (617)495-1000

Holyoke Community College*
Holyoke   (413)538-7000

Marian Court Junior College*
Swampscott   (617)595-6768

Massachusetts College Of Art*
Boston   (617)232-1555

Massachusetts Institute Of
Technology
Cambridge   (617)253-1000

Massachusetts Maritime Academy*
Buzzards Bay   (508)759-5761

Mount Holyoke College
South Hadley   (413)538-2000

Nichols College
Dudley   (508)943-1560

North Adams State College*
North Adams   (413)664-4511

North Shore Community College*
Beverly   (508)922-6722

Northeastern University
Boston   (617)437-2000

*Institution indicates *comprehensive* prior learning assessment available.

Northern Essex Community
College*
Haverhill   (508)374-3900

Pope John XXIII National Seminary
Weston   (617)899-5500

Quinsigamond Community
College*
Worcester   (508)853-2300

Saint Hyacinth College And
Seminary
Granby   (413)467-7191

Simmons College*
Boston   (617)738-2000

Smith College
Northampton   (413)584-2700

Southeastern Massachusetts
University*
North Dartmouth   (508)999-8000

Springfield College*
Springfield   (413)788-3000

Stonehill College
North Easton   (508)238-1081

University Of Lowell
Lowell   (508)934-4000

University Of Massachusetts At
Amherst*
Amherst   (413)545-0111

Wellesley College
Wellesley   (617)235-0320

Wentworth Institute Of
Technology*
Boston   (617)442-9010

Western New England College
Springfield   (413)782-3111

Wheaton College
Norton   (508)260-5000

Worcester State College
Worcester   (508)793-8000

MICHIGAN

Adrian College*
Adrian   (517)265-5161

Alma College
Alma   (517)463-7111

Alpena Community College*
Alpena   (517)356-9021

Baker College Of Owosso*
Owosso   (517)723-5251

Bay De Noc Community College*
Escanaba   (906)786-5802

Central Michigan University
Mount Pleasant   (517)774-3151

Cleary College*
Ypsilanti   (313)483-4400

Concordia College*
Ann Arbor   (313)995-7300

Delta College*
University Center   (517)686-9000

Detroit College Of Business*
Dearborn   (313)581-4400

Eastern Michigan University*
Ypsilanti   (313)487-1849

Ferris State University*
Big Rapids   (616)592-2000

Glen Oaks Community College
Centreville   (616)467-9945

Gogebic Community College*
Ironwood   (906)932-4231

Grace Bible College
Grand Rapids   (616)538-2330

Grand Rapids Baptist College And
Seminary
Grand Rapids   (616)949-5300

Henry Ford Community College
Dearborn   (313)271-2750

*Institution indicates *comprehensive* prior learning assessment available.

Hope College
Holland   (616)392-5111

Jackson Community College*
Jackson   (517)787-0800

Kalamazoo Valley Community
  College*
Kalamazoo   (616)372-5000

Kellogg Community College*
Battle Creek   (616)965-3931

Kendall College Of Art And Design
Grand Rapids   (616)451-2787

Kirtland Community College
Roscommon   (517)275-5121

Lake Michigan College*
Benton Harbor   (616)927-3571

Lake Superior State University
Sault Sainte Marie   (906)632-6841

Madonna College*
Livonia   (313)591-5000

Marygrove College*
Detroit   (313)862-8000

Mercy College Of Detroit*
Detroit   (313)592-6000

Michigan Christian College*
Rochester   (313)651-5800

Michigan State University
East Lansing   (517)355-1855

Michigan Technological University*
Houghton   (906)487-1885

Mid Michigan Community College*
Harrison   (517)386-7792

Montcalm Community College*
Sidney   (517)328-2111

Northwestern Michigan College*
Traverse City   (616)922-0650

Northwood Institute*
Midland   (517)631-1600

Oakland Community College
Bloomfield Hills   (313)540-1500

Oakland University
Rochester   (313)370-2100

Olivet College*
Olivet   (616)749-7000

Sacred Heart Major Seminary/
  College And Theologate*
Detroit   (313)883-8500

Saint Mary's College*
Orchard Lake   (219)284-4000

Schoolcraft College*
Livonia   (313)462-4400

Siena Heights College
Adrian   (517)263-0731

Spring Arbor College*
Spring Arbor   (517)750-1200

Suomi College
Hancock   (906)482-5300

University Of Michigan —
  Ann Arbor
Ann Arbor   (313)764-1817

University Of Michigan — Dearborn
Dearborn   (313)593-5000

University Of Michigan — Flint
Flint   (313)762-3000

Western Michigan University*
Kalamazoo   (616)387-1000

MINNESOTA

Augsburg College*
Minneapolis   (612)330-1000

Austin Community College
Austin   (512)483-7000

Bemidji State University*
Bemidji   (218)755-2000

*Institution indicates *comprehensive* prior learning assessment available.

Bethany Lutheran College
Mankato   (507)625-2977

Brainerd Community College
Brainerd   (218)828-2525

College Of Saint Benedict*
Saint Joseph   (612)363-5011

College Of Saint Catherine*
Saint Paul   (612)690-6000

College Of Saint Scholastica*
Duluth   (218)723-6000

Concordia College-Saint Paul*
Saint Paul   (612)641-8278

Dr. Martin Luther College
New Ulm   (507)354-8221

Dunwoody Industrial Institute
Minneapolis   (612)374-5800

Fergus Falls Community College
Fergus Falls   (218)739-7500

Gustavus Adolphus College
Saint Peter   (507)931-8000

Inver Hills Community College*
Inver Grove Heights (612)450-8500

Metropolitan State University*
Saint Paul   (612)296-3875

Minneapolis Community College*
Minneapolis   (612)341-7000

Minnesota Bible College
Rochester   (507)288-4563

Moorhead State University*
Moorhead   (218)236-2011

North Hennepin Community
  College*
Brooklyn Park   (612)424-0811

Northwestern College*
Roseville   (712)737-4821

Northwestern Electronics Institute
Minneapolis   (612)781-4881

Oak Hills Bible College*
Bemidji   (218)751-8670

Rochester Community College*
Rochester   (507)285-7210

Saint Cloud State University
Saint Cloud   (612)255-0121

Saint John's University
Collegeville   (612)363-2011

Saint Mary's College
Winona   (219)284-4000

Southwest State University
Marshall   (507)537-7021

University Of Minnesota —
  Crookston
Crookston   (218)281-6510

University Of Minnesota — Morris*
Morris   (612)589-2211

University Of Minnesota —
  Twin Cities*
Minneapolis   (612)625-5000

Willmar Community College*
Willmar   (612)231-5102

Winona State University*
Winona   (507)457-5000

Worthington Community College*
Worthington   (507)372-2107

MISSISSIPPI

Belhaven College*
Jackson   (601)968-5919

Delta State University
Cleveland   (601)846-3000

Hinds Community College*
Raymond   (601)857-5261

Itawamba Community College
Fulton   (601)862-3101

*Institution indicates *comprehensive* prior learning assessment available.

Meridian Community College
Meridian   (601)483-8241

Millsaps College*
Jackson   (601)354-5201

Mississippi Delta Community
College
Moorhead   (601)246-5631

Mississippi Gulf Coast Community
College
Perkinston   (601)928-5211

Mississippi University For Women
Columbus   (601)329-7100

Mississippi Valley State University
Itta Bena   (601)254-9041

Pearl River Community College
Poplarville   (601)795-6801

Southwest Mississippi Community
College
Summit   (601)276-2000

University Of Mississippi
University   (601)232-7211

University Of Southern Mississippi*
Hattiesburg   (601)266-4111

William Carey College
Hattiesburg   (601)582-5051

Wood Junior College
Mathiston   (601)263-8128

MISSOURI

Avila College*
Kansas City   (816)942-8400

Central Missouri State University*
Warrensburg   (816)429-4111

College Of The Ozarks
Point Lookout   (417)334-6411

Columbia College*
Columbia   (312)663-1600

Cottey College
Nevada   (417)667-8181

Crowder College
Neosho   (417)451-3223

Culver-Stockton College*
Canton   (314)288-5221

Deaconess College Of Nursing
St. Louis   (314)768-3044

Drury College
Springfield   (417)865-8731

East Central College
Union   (314)583-5193

Evangel College
Springfield   (417)865-2811

Fontbonne College*
Saint Louis   (314)862-3456

Hannibal-La Grange College
Hannibal   (314)221-3675

Jefferson College
Hillsboro   (314)789-3951

Kemper Military School And
College
Boonville   (816)882-5623

Lincoln University
Jefferson City   (314)681-5000

Longview Community College
Lee's Summit   (816)763-7777

Maple Woods Community College
Kansas City   (816)436-6500

Maryville College*
Saint Louis   (314)576-9300

Metropolitan Community College
Kansas City   (816)756-0220

Mineral Area College
Flat River   (314)431-4593

*Institution indicates *comprehensive* prior learning assessment available.

Missouri Southern State College
Joplin (417)625-9300

Moberly Area Community College
Moberly (816)263-4110

North Central Missouri College
Trenton (816)359-3948

Northeast Missouri State University
Kirksville (816)785-4000

Northwest Missouri State University
Maryville (816)562-1212

Rockhurst College
Kansas City (816)926-4000

Saint Louis University*
Saint Louis (314)658-2222

Southeast Missouri State University
Cape Girardeau (314)651-2000

Southwest Missouri State University
Springfield (417)836-5000

St. Charles County Community
College
St. Charles (314)723-1220

State Fair Community College*
Sedalia (816)826-7100

Stephens College*
Columbia (314)442-2211

Tarkio College*
Tarkio (816)736-4131

University Of Missouri — Columbia
Columbia (314)882-2121

University Of Missouri —
Kansas City
Kansas City (816)276-1000

University Of Missouri — Rolla
Rolla (314)341-4111

University Of Missouri —
Saint Louis*
Saint Louis (314)553-5000

Webster University*
Saint Louis (314)968-6900

William Woods College
Fulton (314)642-2251

MONTANA

Carroll College
Helena (406)442-3450

Dawson Community College
Glendive (406)365-3396

Eastern Montana College
Billings (406)657-2011

Flathead Valley Community College
Kalispell (406)752-5222

Miles Community College*
Miles City (406)232-3031

Northern Montana College*
Havre (406)265-3700

Rocky Mountain College*
Billings (406)657-1000

University Of Montana
Missoula (406)243-0211

NEBRASKA

Bishop Clarkson College
Omaha (402)559-3100

Central Community College*
Grand Island (308)384-5220

Chadron State College*
Chadron (308)432-4451

College Of Saint Mary*
Omaha (402)399-2400

Concordia Teachers College
Seward (402)643-3651

*Institution indicates *comprehensive* prior learning assessment available.

Creighton University*
Omaha   (402)280-2700

Dana College*
Blair   (402)426-9000

Doane College*
Crete   (402)826-2161

Hastings College
Hastings   (402)463-2402

Metropolitan Community College*
Omaha   (402)449-8400

Mid-Plains Technical Community
  College Area
North Platte   (308)534-9265

Midland Lutheran College
Fremont   (402)721-5480

Nebraska Wesleyan University
Lincoln   (402)466-2371

Northeast Community College
Norfolk   (402)371-2020

Peru State College
Peru   (402)872-3815

Southeast Community College
Lincoln   (402)471-3303

Union College
Lincoln   (606)546-4151

University Of Nebraska At Omaha
Omaha   (402)554-2200

University Of Nebraska —
  Lincoln*
Lincoln   (402)472-7211

Wayne State College
Wayne   (402)375-2200

York College*
York   (402)362-4441

NEVADA

Northern Nevada Community
  College*
Elko   (702)738-8493

NEW HAMPSHIRE

Castle Junior College*
Windham   (603)893-6111

Colby-Sawyer College*
New London   (603)526-2010

Dartmouth College
Hanover   (603)646-1110

Keene State College*
Keene   (603)352-1909

New England College*
Henniker   (603)428-2211

New Hampshire Technical College
  At Laconia*
Laconia   (603)524-3207
New Hampshire Technical Institute*
Concord   (603)225-1800

Notre Dame College*
Manchester   (603)669-4298

Rivier College*
Nashua   (603)888-1311

Saint Anselm College
Manchester   (603)641-7000

University Of New Hampshire
Durham   (603)862-1234

NEW JERSEY

Atlantic Community College
Mays Landing   (609)343-4900

*Institution indicates *comprehensive* prior learning assessment available.

Bloomfield College*
Bloomfield   (201)748-9000

Burlington County College
Pemberton   (609)894-9311

Centenary College*
Hackettstown   (201)852-1400

College Of Saint Elizabeth
Convent Station   (201)292-6300

Cumberland County College
Vineland   (609)691-8600

Drew University
Madison   (201)408-3000

Fairleigh Dickinson University*
Teaneck   (201)692-2000

Felician College
Lodi   (201)778-1190

Georgian Court College
Lakewood   (201)364-2200

Glassboro State College
Glassboro   (609)863-5000

Middlesex County College
Edison   (201)548-6000

Montclair State College*
Upper Montclair   (201)893-4000

Ocean County College*
Toms River   (201)255-0400

Ramapo College Of New Jersey*
Mahwah   (201)529-7500

Raritan Valley Community College*
Somerville   (201)526-1200

Saint Peter's College*
Jersey City   (201)915-9000

Salem Community College*
Carneys Point   (609)299-2100

Seton Hall University*
South Orange   (201)761-9000

Stockton State College
Pomona   (609)652-1776

Thomas Edison State College*
Trenton   (609)984-1100

University Of Medicine And
  Dentistry Of New Jersey
Newark   (201)456-4300

Warren County Community
  College Commission*
Washington   (201)689-1090

NEW MEXICO

College Of The Southwest*
Hobbs   (505)392-6561

Eastern New Mexico University
Portales   (505)562-1011

New Mexico Highlands University
Las Vegas   (505)454-3552

New Mexico Institute Of Mining
  And Technology
Socorro   (505)835-5011

New Mexico Junior College
Hobbs   (505)392-4510

New Mexico Military Institute
Roswell   (505)622-6250

New Mexico State University
Las Cruces   (505)646-0111

Northern New Mexico Community
  College
El Rito   (505)581-4501

San Juan College*
Farmington   (505)326-3311

Santa Fe Community College*
Santa Fe   (904)395-5000

Western New Mexico University
Silver City   (505)538-6011

*Institution indicates *comprehensive* prior learning assessment available.

NEW YORK

Albany Medical College*
Albany   (518)445-5521

Alfred University
Alfred   (607)871-2111

Boricua College
New York   (212)694-1000

Broome Community College*
Binghamton   (607)771-5000

Cayuga County Community College
Auburn   (315)255-1743

City University Of New York
Bernard M. Baruch College*
New York   (212)447-3000

City University Of New York
Borough Of Manhattan
Community College
New York   (212)618-1600

City University Of New York
College Of Staten Island*
Staten Island   (718)390-7733

City University Of New York
Herbert H. Lehman College*
Bronx   (212)960-8000

City University Of New York
Hunter College
New York   (212)772-4000

City University Of New York John
Jay College Of Criminal Justice*
New York   (212)237-8000

City University Of New York
Queens College*
Flushing   (212)520-7000

Clinton Community College*
Plattsburgh   (518)561-6650

College Of Aeronautics*
Flushing   (718)429-6600

College Of Saint Rose*
Albany   (518)454-5111

Columbia University in the City
Of New York
New York   (212)854-1754

Cooper Union
New York   (212)254-6300

Corning Community College*
Corning   (607)962-9011

D'Youville College
Buffalo   (716)881-3200

Dominican College Of Blauvelt*
Orangeburg   (914)359-7800

Erie Community College North
Campus*
Williamsville   (716)634-0800

Fashion Institute Of Technology
New York   (212)760-7700

Fordham University*
Bronx   (212)579-2000

Genesee Community College*
Batavia   (716)343-0055

Hamilton College
Clinton   (315)859-4011

Hartwick College*
Oneonta   (607)431-4200

Herkimer County Community
College*
Herkimer   (315)866-0300

Hofstra University*
Hempstead   (516)560-6600

Houghton College*
Houghton   (716)567-2211

Hudson Valley Community
College*
Troy   (518)283-1100

Iona College*
New Rochelle   (914)633-2000

*Institution indicates *comprehensive* prior learning assessment available.

Ithaca College
Ithaca   (607)274-3013

Jamestown Community College*
Jamestown   (716)665-5220

Jefferson Community College
Watertown   (315)782-5250

Keuka College*
Keuka Park   (315)536-4411

King's College
Briarcliff Manor   (914)941-7200

Laboratory Institute Of
  Merchandising*
New York   (212)752-1530

Le Moyne College
Syracuse   (315)445-4100

Marymount College*
Tarrytown   (914)631-3200

Marymount Manhattan College*
New York   (212)517-0400

Mohawk Valley Community
  College*
Utica   (315)792-5400

Mount Saint Mary College*
Newburgh   (914)561-0800

Nassau Community College*
Garden City   (516)222-7501

New York Institute Of Technology
  Central Office*
Old Westbury   (516)686-7516

New York Medical College
Valhalla   (914)993-4000

New York School Of Interior Design
New York   (212)753-5365

Niagara University*
Niagara University   (716)285-1212

Orange County Community College
Middletown   (914)344-6222

Pace University New York Campus*
New York   (212)346-1200

Paul Smith's College Of Arts And
  Sciences
Paul Smiths   (518)327-6211

Phillip Beth Israel School Of
  Nursing
New York   (212)614-6104

Rensselaer Polytechnic Institute
Troy   (518)276-6000

Roberts Wesleyan College*
Rochester   (716)594-9471

Rochester Institute Of Technology*
Rochester   (716)475-24005

Rockland Community College*
Suffern   (914)356-4650

Russell Sage College*
Troy   (518)270-2000

Saint Joseph's College, New York*
Brooklyn   (718)636-6800

Sarah Lawrence College
Bronxville   (914)395-0700

Schenectady County Community
  College*
Schenectady   (518)346-6211

Siena College
Loudonville   (518)783-2300

Skidmore College
Saratoga Springs   (518)584-5000

St. Elizabeth Hospital School Of
  Nursing
Utica   (315)798-8125

St. John Fisher College
Rochester   (716)385-8000

St. Joseph's Hospital Health
  Center School Of Nursing
Syracuse   (315)448-5040

*Institution indicates *comprehensive* prior learning assessment available.

State University Of New York At
 Albany
Albany   (518)442-3300

State University Of New York At
 Buffalo
Buffalo   (716)831-2000

State University Of New York At
 Stony Brook
Stony Brook   (516)689-6000

State University Of New York
 College At Buffalo*
Buffalo   (716)878-4000

State University Of New York
 College At Fredonia*
Fredonia   (716)673-3111

State University Of New York
 College At Geneseo
Geneseo   (716)245-5211

State University Of New York
 College At Oneonta*
Oneonta   (607)431-3500

State University Of New York
 College At Oswego*
Oswego   (315)341-2500

State University Of New York
 College At Potsdam
Potsdam   (315)267-2000

State University Of New York
 College At Purchase*
Purchase   (914)251-6000

State University Of New York
 College Of Agriculture And
 Technology
Morrisville   (315)684-6000

State University Of New York
 College Of Agriculture And
 Technology
Cobleskill   (518)234-5011

State University Of New York
 College Of Technology At Alfred
Alfred   (607)587-4111

State University Of New York
 College Of Technology At Canton*
Canton   (315)386-7011

State University Of New York
 College Of Technology — Delhi*
Delhi   (607)746-4111

State University Of New York
 College Of Technology At
 Utica — Rome
Utica   (315)792-7100

State University Of New York
 Empire State College*
Saratoga Springs   (518)587-2100

State University Of New York
 Maritime College Fort Schuyler
Bronx   (212)409-7200

Suffolk County Community
 College Ammerman Campus*
Selden   (516)451-4110

Sullivan County Community
 College*
Loch Sheldrake   (914)434-5750

Syracuse University Main Campus*
Syracuse   (315)443-1870

Touro College*
New York   (212)447-0700

Ulster County Community College*
Stone Ridge   (914)687-7621

Vassar College
Poughkeepsie   (914)437-7000

Villa Maria College Of Buffalo
Buffalo   (716)896-0700

Wadhams Hall Seminary And
 College
Ogdensburg   (315)393-4231

*Institution indicates *comprehensive* prior learning assessment available.

Wells College
Aurora   (315)364-3370

Westchester Community College
Valhalla   (914)285-6600

NORTH CAROLINA

Asheville-Buncombe Technical
  Community College
Asheville   (704)254-1921

Barton College
Wilson   (919)237-3161

Beaufort County Community
  College
Washington   (919)946-6194

Belmont Abbey College*
Belmont   (704)825-6700

Blue Ridge Community College
Flat Rock   (704)692-3572

Caldwell Community College And
  Technical Institute
Lenoir   (704)726-2200

Cape Fear Community College
Wilmington   (919)343-0481

Carteret Community College
Morehead City   (919)247-6000

Catawba College*
Salisbury   (704)637-4111

Coastal Carolina Community
  College
Jacksonville   (919)455-1221

College Of The Albemarle
Elizabeth City   (919)335-0821

Craven Community College
New Bern   (919)638-4131

Davidson County Community
  College*
Lexington   (704)249-8186

Duke University
Durham   (919)684-8111

Durham Technical Community
  College
Durham   (919)598-9222

East Carolina University
Greenville   (919)757-6131

East Coast Bible College*
Charlotte   (704)394-2307

Elizabeth City State University
Elizabeth City   (919)335-3230

Fayetteville State University
Fayetteville   (919)486-1111

Forsyth Technical Community
  College
Winston-Salem   (919)723-0371

Greensboro College*
Greensboro   (919)272-7102

Guilford College
Greensboro   (919)292-5511

High Point College*
High Point   (919)841-9000

Isothermal Community College*
Spindale   (704)286-3636

James Sprunt Community College*
Kenansville   (919)296-1341

John Wesley College
High Point   (919)889-2262

Johnson C. Smith University
Charlotte   (704)378-1000

Johnston Community College
Smithfield   (919)934-3051

Lees-McRae College
Banner Elk   (704)898-5241

Lenoir-Rhyne College
Hickory   (704)328-1741

Livingstone College*
Salisbury   (704)638-5500

*Institution indicates *comprehensive* prior learning assessment available.

Mars Hill College*
Mars Hill   (704)689-1111

Mayland Community College*
Spruce Pine   (704)765-7351

Mitchell Community College
Statesville   (704)878-3200

Montgomery Community College
Troy   (919)572-3691

Montreat-Anderson College
Montreat   (704)669-8011

Mount Olive College*
Mount Olive   (919)658-2502

North Carolina Central
  University*
Durham   (919)560-6100

North Carolina School Of The
  Arts*
Winston-Salem   (919)770-3399

North Carolina State University
Raleigh   (919)737-2011

North Carolina Wesleyan College
Rocky Mount   (919)977-7171

Pembroke State University
Pembroke   (919)521-4214

Pfeiffer College*
Misenheimer   (704)463-7343

Piedmont Bible College
Winston-Salem   (919)725-8344

Pitt Community College*
Greenville   (919)756-3130

Queens College
Charlotte   (704)337-2200

Randolph Community College*
Asheboro   (919)629-1471

Roanoke-Chowan Community
  College
Ahoskie   (919)332-5921

Rowan-Cabarrus Community
  College*
Salisbury   (704)637-0760

St. Andrews Presbyterian College
Laurinburg   (919)276-3652

University Of North Carolina At
  Asheville
Asheville   (704)251-6600

University Of North Carolina At
  Charlotte
Charlotte   (704)547-2000

University Of North Carolina At
  Greensboro
Greensboro   (919)334-5000

Vance-Granville Community College
Henderson   (919)492-2061

Wake Forest University
Winston-Salem   (919)759-5000

Warren Wilson College*
Swannanoa   (704)298-3325

Wayne Community College
Goldsboro   (919)735-5151

Western Carolina University*
Cullowhee   (704)227-7211

Western Piedmont Community
  College
Morganton   (704)438-6000

Wilkes Community College
Wilkesboro   (919)651-8600

Wingate College
Wingate   (704)233-8000

Winston-Salem State University
Winston-Salem   (919)750-2000

NORTH DAKOTA

Bismarck State Community College
Bismarck   (701)224-5400

*Institution indicates *comprehensive* prior learning assessment available.

Dickinson State University*
Dickinson   (701)227-2507

Fort Bethold Community College
New Town   (701)627-3665

Jamestown College*
Jamestown   (701)252-3467

Medcenter One College Of
  Nursing*
Bismark   (701)224-6732

University Of Mary*
Bismarck   (701)255-7500

University Of North Dakota —
  Lake Region*
Devils Lake   (701)662-8683

University Of North Dakota —
  Main Campus*
Grand Forks   (701)777-2011

Valley City State University*
Valley City   (701)845-7102

OHIO

Antioch University*
Yellow Springs   (513)767-7331

Ashland University
Ashland   (419)289-4142

Baldwin-Wallace College*
Berea   (216)826-2900

Bluffton College
Bluffton   (419)358-8015

Bowling Green State University
  Main Campus*
Bowling Green   (419)372-2531

Capital University*
Columbus   (614)236-6011

Chatfield College*
Saint Martin   (513)875-3344

Cincinnati Bible College And
  Seminary
Cincinnati   (513)244-8100

Clark State Community College*
Springfield   (513)325-0691

Cleveland Institute Of Art
Cleveland   (216)229-0900

Cleveland State University
Cleveland   (216)687-2000

College Of Mount Saint Joseph*
Mount Saint Joseph (513)244-4200

Columbus State Community
  College
Columbus   (614)227-2400

Cuyahoga Community College
Cleveland   (216)987-4000

Davis College
Toledo   (419)473-2700

Denison University
Granville   (614)587-0810

Dyke College*
Cleveland   (216)696-9000

Edison State Community College*
Piqua   (513)778-8600

Franciscan University Of
  Steubenville*
Steubenville   (614)283-3771

Franklin University*
Columbus   (614)224-6237

Heidelberg College*
Tiffin   (419)448-2000

Jefferson Technical College
Steubenville   (614)264-5591

John Carroll University
Cleveland   (216)397-1886

Kent State University —
  Ashtabula Campus
Ashtabula   (216)964-3322

*Institution indicates *comprehensive* prior learning assessment available.

Kent State University —
East Liverpool Campus
East Liverpool   (216)385-3805

Kent State University —
Main Campus*
Kent   (216)672-2121

Kent State University —
Tuscarawas Campus
New Philadelphia   (216)339-3391

Kenyon College
Gambier   (614)427-5000

Lakeland Community College*
Mentor   (216)953-7000

Lima Technical College*
Lima   (419)222-8324

Lorain County Community
College*
Elyria   (216)365-4191

Lourdes College*
Sylvania   (419)885-3211

Malone College*
Canton   (216)489-0800

Marietta College*
Marietta   (614)373-4643

Marion Technical College
Marion   (614)389-4636

Miami University
Oxford   (513)529-1809

Miami University Hamilton Campus
Hamilton   (513)863-8833

Miami University Middletown
Campus
Middletown   (513)424-4444

Mount Union College*
Alliance   (216)821-5320

Muskingum Area Technical College*
Zanesville   (614)454-2501

Muskingum College*
New Concord   (614)826-8211

North Central Technical College*
Mansfield   (419)755-4800

Northwestern Business College —
Technical Center
Lima   (419)227-3141

Notre Dame College*
Cleveland   (603)669-4298

Ohio Northern University
Ada   (419)772-2000

Ohio University Central Office*
Athens   (614)593-1000

Ohio University — Chillicothe
Campus*
Chillicothe   (614)774-7200

Ohio Wesleyan University
Delaware   (614)369-4431

Owens Technical College
Toledo   (419)666-0580

Pontifical College Josephinum
Columbus   (614)885-5585

Shawnee State University
Portsmouth   (614)354-3205

Sinclair Community College*
Dayton   (513)226-2500

Southern Ohio College
Cincinnati   (513)242-3791

Southern State Community College*
Hillsboro   (513)393-3431

Stark Technical College*
Canton   (216)494-6170

The Defiance College*
Defiance   (419)784-4010

The Ohio State University
Main Campus
Columbus   (614)292-6446

*Institution indicates *comprehensive* prior learning assessment available.

Union Institute*
Cincinnati   (513)861-6400

University Of Akron Main
  Campus
Akron   (216)972-7100

University Of Cincinnati
  Main Campus*
Cincinnati   (513)556-6000

University Of Cincinnati —
  Clermont College*
Batavia   (513)732-5200

University Of Dayton
Dayton   (513)229-1000

University Of Rio Grande*
Rio Grande   (614)245-5353

University Of Toledo*
Toledo   (419)537-4242

Urbana University*
Urbana   (513)652-1301

Ursuline College*
Cleveland   (216)449-4200

Walsh College*
Canton   (216)499-7090

Washington Technical College*
Marietta   (614)374-8716

Wilmington College*
Wilmington   (513)382-6661

Wittenberg University
Springfield   (513)327-6231

Wright State University Main
  Campus
Dayton   (513)873-3333

Xavier University
Cincinnati   (513)745-3000

Youngstown State University
Youngstown   (216)742-3000

OKLAHOMA

Cameron University
Lawton   (405)581-2200

Central State University*
Edmond   (513)376-6011

East Central University*
Ada   (405)332-8000

Langston University
Langston   (405)466-2231

Murray State College*
Tishomingo   (405)371-2371

Northeastern State University
Tahlequah   (918)456-5511

Oklahoma Baptist University
Shawnee   (405)275-2850

Oklahoma Christian University of
  Science & Arts
Oklahoma City   (405)425-5000

Oklahoma City Community
  College*
Oklahoma City   (405)682-1611

Oklahoma City University*
Oklahoma City   (405)521-5000

Oklahoma Panhandle State
  University
Goodwell   (405)349-2611

Phillips University
Enid   (405)237-4433

Rose State College
Midwest City   (405)733-7311

Southern Nazarene University*
Bethany   (405)789-6400

Southwestern Oklahoma State
  University
Weatherford   (405)772-6611

*Institution indicates *comprehensive* prior learning assessment available.

University Of Oklahoma Norman
Campus
Norman   (405)325-0311

University Of Science And Arts
Of Oklahoma
Chickasha   (405)224-3140

University Of Tulsa
Tulsa   (918)631-2000

Western Oklahoma State College*
Altus   (405)477-2000

OREGON

Blue Mountain Community College*
Pendleton   (503)276-1260

Central Oregon Community College
Bend   (503)382-6112

Clackamas Community College*
Oregon City   (503)657-8400

Clatsop Community College*
Astoria   (503)325-0910

Columbia Christian College
Portland   (503)255-7060

Eastern Oregon State College*
La Grande   (503)962-2171

George Fox College*
Newberg   (503)538-8383

Lane Community College*
Eugene   (503)747-4501

Lewis And Clark College
Portland   (503)768-7000

Linfield College*
McMinnville   (503)472-4121

Marylhurst College For Lifelong
Learning*
Marylhurst   (503)636-8141

Mt. Hood Community College
Gresham   (503)667-6422

Northwest Christian College*
Eugene   (503)343-1641

Oregon College Of Oriental
Medicine
Portland   (503)253-3443

Oregon Institute Of Technology
Klamath Falls   (503)885-1000

Pacific University
Forest Grove   (503)357-6151

Portland Community College
Portland   (503)244-6111

Portland State University
Portland   (503)725-3000

Rogue Community College*
Grants Pass   (503)479-5541

Southern Oregon State College*
Ashland   (503)482-3311

Umpqua Community College*
Roseburg   (503)440-4600

University Of Oregon
Eugene   (503)346-3111

University Of Portland
Portland   (503)283-7911

Western Oregon State College*
Monmouth   (503)838-8000

Willamette University
Salem   (503)370-6300

PENNSYLVANIA

Albright College*
Reading   (215)921-2381

Allentown College Of Saint
Francis De Sales*
Center Valley   (215)282-1100

*Institution indicates *comprehensive* prior learning assessment available.

Alvernia College*
Reading   (215)777-5411

Art Institute Of Pittsburgh
Pittsburgh   (412)263-6600

Beaver College*
Glenside   (215)572-2900

Bryn Mawr College
Bryn Mawr   (215)526-5000

Bucknell University
Lewisburg   (717)523-1271

Cabrini College*
Radnor   (215)971-8100

California University Of
   Pennsylvania
California   (412)938-4000

Carlow College*
Pittsburgh   (412)578-6000

Carnegie Mellon University
Pittsburgh   (412)268-2000

Central Pennsylvania Business
   School*
Summerdale   (717)732-0702

Chatham College*
Pittsburgh   (412)365-1100

College Misericordia*
Dallas   (717)674-6400

Community College Of Allegheny
   County Allegheny Campus
Pittsburgh   (412)237-2525

Community College Of Allegheny
   County Boyce Campus
Monroeville   (412)327-1327

Community College Of Allegheny
   County College Center-North
Pittsburgh   (412)931-8500

Community College Of Allegheny
   County College Office
Pittsburgh   (412)323-2323

Community College Of Beaver
   County
Monaca   (412)775-8561

Delaware County Community
   College*
Media   (215)359-5000

Delaware Valley College
Doylestown   (215)345-1500

Dickinson College
Carlisle   (717)243-5121

Duquesne University*
Pittsburgh   (412)434-6000

East Stroudsburg University Of
   Pennsylvania
East Stroudsburg   (717)424-3547

Eastern College*
Saint Davids   (215)341-5810

Edinboro University Of
   Pennsylvania*
Edinboro   (814)732-2000

Elizabethtown College*
Elizabethtown   (717)367-1151

Franklin And Marshall College
Lancaster   (717)291-3911

Gannon University*
Erie   (814)871-7000

Geneva College*
Beaver Falls   (412)846-5100

Gettysburg College
Gettysburg   (717)337-6000

Grove City College
Grove City   (412)458-2000

Holy Family College*
Philadelphia   (215)637-7700

ICS Center For Degree Studies
Scranton   (717)342-7701

Immaculata College
Immaculata   (215)647-4400

*Institution indicates *comprehensive* prior learning assessment available.

King's College*
Wilkes-Barre   (914)941-7200

Kutztown University Of
  Pennsylvania
Kutztown   (215)683-4000

La Roche College*
Pittsburgh   (412)367-9300

La Salle University*
Philadelphia   (215)951-1000

Lackawanna Junior College*
Scranton   (717)961-7810

Lafayette College
Easton   (215)250-5000

Lancaster Bible College
Lancaster   (717)569-7071

Lebanon Valley College*
Annville   (717)867-6100

Lehigh County Community
  College*
Schnecksville   (215)799-2121

Lehigh University
Bethlehem   (215)758-3000

Luzerne County Community
  College*
Nanticoke   (717)735-8300

Marywood College*
Scranton   (717)348-6211

Montgomery County Community
  College*
Blue Bell   (215)641-6300

Muhlenberg College
Allentown   (215)821-3000

Neumann College*
Aston   (215)459-0905

Northampton County Area
  Community College
Bethlehem   (215)861-5300

Northeastern Christian Junior
  College*
Villanova   (215)525-6780

Peirce Junior College
Philadelphia   (215)545-6400

Pennsylvania State University
  Main Campus
University Park   (814)865-4700

Pennsylvania State University
  McKeesport Campus
McKeesport   (412)675-9000

Philadelphia College Of Textiles
  And Science
Philadelphia   (215)951-2700

Point Park College*
Pittsburgh   (412)391-4100

Reading Area Community College*
Reading   (215)372-4721

Robert Morris College
Coraopolis   (312)836-4888

Saint Charles Borromeo Seminary
Overbrook   (215)667-3394

Saint Francis College
Loretto   (219)432-3551

Seton Hill College*
Greensburg   (412)834-2200

Slippery Rock University Of
  Pennsylvania
Slippery Rock   (412)738-0512

Susquehanna University
Selinsgrove   (717)374-0101

Swarthmore College
Swarthmore   (215)328-8000

Tracey-Warner School
Philadelphia   (215)574-0402

University Of Pittsburgh At
  Bradford
Bradford   (814)362-7500

*Institution indicates *comprehensive* prior learning assessment available.

University Of Pittsburgh
Main Campus
Pittsburgh   (412)624-4141

University Of Scranton*
Scranton   (717)964-7400

University Of The Arts
Philadelphia   (215)875-4800

Ursinus College
Collegeville   (215)489-4111

Valley Forge Christian College
Phoenixville   (215)935-0450

Waynesburg College*
Waynesburg   (412)627-8191

West Chester University Of
Pennsylvania*
West Chester   (215)436-1000

Westminster College*
New Wilmington   (314)642-3361

Westmoreland County Community
College*
Youngwood   (412)925-4000

Widener University*
Chester   (215)499-4000

Wilson College*
Chambersburg   (717)264-4141

PUERTO RICO

Antillian College
Mayaguez   (809)834-9595

Bayamon Central University
Bayamon   (809)786-3030

Inter American University Of Puerto
Rico Fajardo Regional College*
Fajardo   (809)863-2390

Inter American University Of Puerto
Rico Metropolitan Campus*
Hato Rey   (809)758-8000

Universidad Metropolitana
Rio Piedras   (809)751-0178

University Of Puerto Rico
Carolina Regional College
Carolina   (809)257-0000

University Of Puerto Rico
Humacao University College
Humacao   (809)850-0000

University Of Puerto Rico
Mayaguez Campus Post
Mayaguez   (809)832-4040

RHODE ISLAND

Bryant College
Smithfield   (401)232-6000

Rhode Island School Of Design
Providence   (401)331-3511

Roger Williams College*
Bristol   (401)253-1040

Salve Regina College*
Newport   (401)847-6650

SOUTH CAROLINA

Aiken Technical College*
Aiken   (803)593-9231

Benedict College
Columbia   (803)256-4220

Bob Jones University
Greenville   (803)242-5100

Clemson University
Clemson   (803)656-3311

Coker College*
Hartsville   (803)332-1381

Columbia Bible College And
Seminary
Columbia   (803)754-4100

*Institution indicates *comprehensive* prior learning assessment available.

Columbia College*
Columbia   (312)663-1600

Denmark Technical College*
Denmark   (803)793-3301

Erskine College
Due West   (803)379-2131

Francis Marion College
Florence   (803)661-1362

Furman University
Greenville   (803)294-2000

Greenville Technical College*
Greenville   (803)250-8000

Lander College
Greenwood   (803)229-8300

Limestone College
Gaffney   (803)489-7151
Newberry College
Newberry   (803)276-5010

Orangeburg-Calhoun Technical
College
Orangeburg   (803)536-0311

Presbyterian College
Clinton   (803)833-2820

Spartanburg Methodist College
Spartanburg   (803)587-4000

Sumter Area Technical College*
Sumter   (803)778-1961

Technical College Of The
Lowcountry*
Beaufort   (803)525-8324

Trident Technical College
Charleston   (803)572-6111

University Of South Carolina —
Aiken
Aiken   (803)648-6851

University Of South Carolina —
Coastal Carolina
Conway   (803)347-3161

University Of South Carolina —
Columbia
Columbia   (803)777-0411

University Of South Carolina —
Salkehatchie
Allendale   (803)584-3446

University Of South Carolina —
Spartanburg
Spartanburg   (803)578-1800

University Of South Carolina —
Sumter
Sumter   (803)775-6341

Wofford College
Spartanburg   (803)585-4821

York Technical College*
Rock Hill   (803)327-8000

SOUTH DAKOTA

Augustana College*
Sioux Falls   (309)794-7000

Black Hills State University*
Spearfish   (605)642-6011

Dakota Wesleyan University*
Mitchell   (605)995-2600

Huron University*
Huron   (605)352-8721

Kilian Community College*
Sioux Falls   (605)336-1711

Mitchell Vocational — Technical
School*
Mitchell   (605)995-3024

National College*
Rapid City   (605)394-4800

Northern State University
Aberdeen   (605)622-3011

*Institution indicates *comprehensive* prior learning assessment available.

Presentation College
Aberdeen   (605)225-0420

Sioux Falls College*
Sioux Falls   (605)331-5000

South Dakota School Of Mines
  And Technology
Rapid City   (605)394-2511

South Dakota State University
Brookings   (605)688-4151

TENNESSEE

Aquinas Junior College
Nashville   (615)297-7545

Austin Peay State University
Clarksville   (615)648-7011

Bethel College*
McKenzie   (219)259-8511

Carson-Newman College*
Jefferson City   (615)475-9061

Christian Brothers University
Memphis   (901)722-0200

Cleveland State Community
  College
Cleveland   (615)472-7141

Cumberland University*
Lebanon   (615)444-2562

Dyersburg State Community
  College*
Dyersburg   (901)286-3200

East Tennessee State University*
Johnson City   (615)929-4112

Freed-Hardeman University
Henderson   (901)989-6000

Hiwassee College
Madisonville   (615)442-2091

King College
Bristol   (615)968-1187

Lambuth College
Jackson   (901)425-2500

Lincoln Memorial University*
Harrogate   (615)869-3611

Middle Tennessee State University
Murfreesboro   (615)898-2300

Milligan College*
Milligan College   (615)929-0116

Motlow State Community College
Tullahoma   (615)455-8511

Nashville State Technical Institute*
Nashville   (615)353-3333

Northeast State Technical
  Community College
Blountville   (615)323-3191

Rhodes College
Memphis   (901)726-3000

Roane State Community College*
Harriman   (615)354-3000

Shelby State Community College*
Memphis   (901)528-6700

Southern College Of Seventh-Day
  Adventists
Collegedale   (615)238-2111

State Technical Institute At
  Memphis*
Memphis   (901)377-4111

Tennessee Technological University
Cookeville   (615)372-3101

Tennessee Wesleyan College
Athens   (615)745-7504

Tomlinson College*
Cleveland   (615)476-3271

Trevecca Nazarene College*
Nashville   (615)248-1200

Tusculum College*
Greeneville   (615)636-7300

*Institution indicates *comprehensive* prior learning assessment available.

Union University
Jackson   (901)668-1818

University Of Tennessee At
  Chattanooga*
Chattanooga   (615)755-4141

University Of Tennessee At Martin
Martin   (901)587-7000

University Of Tennessee Central
  Office
Knoxville   (615)974-1000

Vanderbilt University
Nashville   (615)322-7311

Walters State Community College
Morristown   (615)587-9722

TEXAS

Abilene Christian University
Abilene   (915)674-2000

Alvin Community College*
Alvin   (713)331-6111

Amarillo College*
Amarillo   (806)371-5000
Angelina College
Lufkin   (409)639-1301

Austin College
Sherman   (214)813-2000

Brazosport College
Lake Jackson   (409)265-6131

Cedar Valley College*
Lancaster   (214)372-8200

Central Texas College*
Killeen   (817)526-1211

Concordia Lutheran College*
Austin   (512)452-7661

Dallas Baptist University*
Dallas   (214)331-8311

Dallas Theological Seminary
Dallas   (214)824-3094

Del Mar College
Corpus Christi   (512)886-1200

East Texas Baptist University*
Marshall   (214)935-7963

East Texas State University*
Commerce   (214)886-5014

Eastfield College*
Mesquite   (214)324-7100

El Centro College*
Dallas   (214)746-2200

Frank Phillips College
Borger   (806)274-5311

Hallmark Institute Of Technology
San Antonio   (512)924-8551

Hardin-Simmons University
Abilene   (915)670-1000

Houston Community College*
Houston   (713)869-5021

Howard Payne University*
Brownwood   (915)643-2502

Jarvis Christian College
Hawkins   (214)769-2174

Lamar University — Beaumont*
Beaumont   (409)880-7011

Laredo Junior College
Laredo   (512)722-0521

LeTourneau University*
Longview   (214)753-0231

Lubbock Christian University
Lubbock   (806)792-3221

McMurry College
Abilene   (915)691-6200

Midland College
Midland   (915)685-4500

*Institution indicates *comprehensive* prior learning assessment available.

Midwestern State University*
Wichita Falls   (817)692-6611

North Harris County College
Houston   (713)591-3500

Northeast Texas Community
  College*
Mount Pleasant   (214)572-1911

Paris Junior College*
Paris   (214)785-7661

Prairie View A & M University
Prairie View   (409)857-3311

Richland College
Dallas   (214)238-6194

Sam Houston State University
Huntsville   (409)294-1111

San Antonio Art Institute
San Antonio   (512)824-7224

San Jacinto College Central Campus
Pasadena   (713)476-1501

Schreiner College*
Kerrville   (512)896-5411

Southwest Texas Junior College
Uvalde   (512)278-4401

Southwest Texas State University*
San Marcos   (512)245-2111

Southwestern Adventist College*
Keene   (817)645-3921

Southwestern Assemblies Of God
  College*
Waxahachie   (214)937-4010

Southwestern University
Georgetown   (512)863-6511

St. Edward's University*
Austin   (512)448-8400

St. Mary's University
San Antonio   (512)436-3722

St. Philip's College
San Antonio   (512)531-3200

Stephen F. Austin State University*
Nacogdoches   (409)568-2201

Tarrant County Junior College*
Fort Worth   (817)336-7851

Texas A & M University System
  Office
College Station   (409)845-4331

Texas State Technical Institute —
  Amarillo
Amarillo   (806)335-2316

Texas Woman's University
Denton   (817)898-3201

Trinity University
San Antonio   (512)736-7011

Trinity Valley Community College
Athens   (214)677-8822

Tyler Junior College*
Tyler   (214)510-2200

University Of Central Texas*
Killeen   (817)526-1150

University Of Dallas
Irving   (214)721-5000

University Of Houston —
  Clear Lake
Houston   (713)488-7170

University Of Mary Hardin —
  Baylor
Belton   (817)939-8642

University Of North Texas*
Denton   (817)565-2000

University Of Saint Thomas
Houston   (713)522-7911

University Of Texas At Dallas
Richardson   (214)690-2111

University Of Texas At El Paso
El Paso   (915)747-5000

University Of Texas At San Antonio
San Antonio   (512)691-4011

*Institution indicates *comprehensive* prior learning assessment available.

University Of Texas Health
Science Center At Houston
Houston   (713)792-4975

Vernon Regional Junior College
Vernon   (817)552-6291

Wayland Baptist University*
Plainview   (806)296-5521

Wharton County Junior College
Wharton   (409)532-4560

UTAH

Brigham Young University
Provo   (801)378-1211

Latter-Day Saints Business College
Salt Lake City   (801)363-2765

Salt Lake Community College
Salt Lake City   (801)967-4111

Snow College
Ephraim   (801)283-4021

University Of Utah
Salt Lake City   (801)581-7200

Utah Valley Community College*
Provo   (801)222-8000

Westminster College Of Salt Lake
City*
Salt Lake City   (801)484-7651

VERMONT

Burlington College*
Burlington   (802)862-9616

Castleton State College*
Castleton   (802)468-5611

Community College Of Vermont*
Waterbury   (802)241-3535

Goddard College
Plainfield   (802)454-8311

Green Mountain College
Poultney   (802)287-9313

Lyndon State College*
Lyndonville   (802)626-9371

Marlboro College
Marlboro   (802)257-4333

Middlebury College
Middlebury   (802)388-3711

Saint Michael's College
Colchester   (802)655-2000

Trinity College*
Burlington   (203)297-2000

VIRGIN ISLANDS

University Of The Virgin Islands
Saint Thomas   (809)776-9200

VIRGINIA

Averett College*
Danville   (804)791-5600

Blue Ridge Community College*
Weyers Cave   (704)692-3572

Bluefield College*
Bluefield   (703)326-3682

Bridgewater College
Bridgewater   (703)828-2501

Central Virginia Community
College*
Lynchburg   (804)386-4500

Commonwealth College
Virginia Beach   (804)625-5891

---

*Institution indicates *comprehensive* prior learning assessment available.

Community Hospital Of Roanoke
Valley College Of Health Sciences
Roanoke   (703)985-8483

Dabney S. Lancaster Community
College
Clifton Forge   (703)862-4246

Eastern Shore Community College
Melfa   (804)787-5900

Emory And Henry College
Emory   (703)944-3121

George Mason University*
Fairfax   (703)323-2000

Hampden-Sydney College
Hampden-Sydney   (804)223-4381

Hollins College
Hollins College   (703)362-6000

J. Sargeant Reynolds Community
College
Richmond   (804)371-3200

James Madison University
Harrisonburg   (703)568-6211

John Tyler Community College*
Chester   (804)796-4000

Liberty University*
Lynchburg   (804)582-2000

Lynchburg College
Lynchburg   (804)522-8100

Mary Washington College*
Fredericksburg   (703)899-4100

Marymount University
Arlington   (703)522-5600

New River Community College*
Dublin   (703)674-3600

Northern Virginia Community
College*
Annandale   (703)323-3000

Old Dominion University*
Norfolk   (804)683-3000

Paul D. Camp Community
College*
Franklin   (804)562-2171

Piedmont Virginia Community
College*
Charlottesville   (804)977-3900

Rappahannock Community College
Glenns   (804)758-5324

Richard Bland College Of The
College Of William And Mary*
Petersburg   (804)862-6100

Roanoke College
Salem   (703)375-2500

Shenandoah University
Winchester   (703)665-4506

Southern Seminary College
Buena Vista   (703)261-8400

Southside Virginia Community
College
Alberta   (804)949-7111

Thomas Nelson Community
College
Hampton   (804)825-2700

University Of Richmond
Richmond   (804)289-8000

Virginia Highlands Community
College*
Abingdon   (703)628-6094

Virginia Intermont College*
Bristol   (703)669-6101

Virginia Military Institute
Lexington   (703)464-7311

Virginia Polytechnic Institute And
State University
Blacksburg   (703)231-6000

Virginia State University*
Petersburg   (804)524-5000

Virginia Union University*
Richmond   (804)257-5600

*Institution indicates *comprehensive* prior learning assessment available.

Virginia Wesleyan College*
Norfolk   (804)461-3232

Washington And Lee University
Lexington   (703)463-8400

WASHINGTON

Big Bend Community College*
Moses Lake   (509)762-5351

Central Washington University
Ellensburg   (509)963-1111

Centralia College
Centralia   (206)736-9391

Columbia Basin College
Pasco   (509)547-0511

Cornish College Of The Arts
Seattle   (206)323-1400

Eastern Washington University
Cheney   (509)359-2371

Edmonds Community College*
Lynnwood   (206)771-1500

Evergreen State College*
Olympia   (206)866-6000

Gonzaga University
Spokane   (509)328-4220

Grays Harbor College
Aberdeen   (206)532-9020

Green River Community College
Auburn   (206)833-9111

Griffin College
Seattle   (206)728-6800
Heritage College*
Toppenish   (509)865-2244

Lutheran Bible Institute Of Seattle
Issaquah   (206)392-0400

North Seattle Community College*
Seattle   (206)527-3600

Northwest College Of Art
Poulso   (206)779-9993

Northwest Indian College
Bellingham   (206)676-2772

Pacific Lutheran University*
Tacoma   (206)531-6900

Pierce College
Tacoma   (206)964-6500

Saint Martin's College*
Lacey   (206)491-4700

Seattle Pacific University
Seattle   (206)281-2050

South Puget Sound Community
  College*
Olympia   (206)754-7711

South Seattle Community College
Seattle   (206)764-5300

Spokane Community College
Spokane   (509)536-7000

Tacoma Community College
Tacoma   (206)566-5000

University Of Puget Sound
Tacoma   (206)756-3100

Walla Walla College*
College Place   (509)527-2615

Walla Walla Community College
Walla Walla   (509)522-2500

Washington State University
Pullman   (509)335-3564

Whatcom Community College*
Bellingham   (206)676-2170

Whitworth College
Spokane   (509)466-1000

Yakima Valley Community College
Yakima   (509)575-2350

*Institution indicates *comprehensive* prior learning assessment available.

WEST VIRGINIA

Alderson Broaddus College
Philippi   (304) 457-1700

Bethany College*
Bethany   (408) 438-3800

Bluefield State College*
Bluefield   (304) 327-4000

Davis & Elkins College*
Elkins   (304) 636-1900

Fairmont State College*
Fairmont   (304) 367-4000

Glenville State College*
Glenville   (304) 462-7361

Salem-Teikyo University*
Salem   (304) 782-5011

University Of Charleston*
Charleston   (304) 357-4800

West Liberty State College*
West Liberty   (304) 336-5000

West Virginia Institute Of
  Technology*
Montgomery   (304) 442-3071

West Virginia Northern Community
  College
Wheeling   (304) 233-5900

West Virginia State College*
Institute   (304) 766-3000

West Virginia University*
Morgantown   (304) 293-0111

West Virginia University At
  Parkersburg
Parkersburg   (304) 424-8000

Wheeling Jesuit College*
Wheeling   (304) 243-2000

WISCONSIN

Bellin College Of Nursing*
Green Bay   (414) 433-3560

Beloit College*
Beloit   (608) 363-2000

Cardinal Stritch College*
Milwaukee   (414) 352-5400

Carthage College
Kenosha   (414) 551-8500

Columbia College Of Nursing
Milwaukee   (414) 961-3530

Concordia University, Wisconsin*
Mequon   (414) 243-5700

Edgewood College*
Madison   (608) 257-4861

Gateway Technical College*
Kenosha   (414) 656-6900

Lawrence University
Appleton   (414) 832-7000

Madison Area Technical College*
Madison   (608) 246-6282

Maranatha Baptist Bible College
Watertown   (414) 261-9300

Marian College Of Fond Du Lac*
Fond Du Lac   (414) 923-7600

Milwaukee Area Technical College*
Milwaukee   (414) 278-6600

Moraine Park Technical College*
Fond Du Lac   (414) 922-8611

Mount Mary College*
Milwaukee   (414) 258-4810

Northcentral Technical College*
Wausau   (715) 675-3331

Northeast Wisconsin Technical
  College
Green Bay   (414) 498-5400

*Institution indicates *comprehensive* prior learning assessment available.

Northland College*
Ashland   (715)682-1699

Northwestern College
Watertown   (712)737-4821

Ripon College
Ripon   (414)748-8115

Saint Norbert College*
De Pere   (414)337-3181

Silver Lake College*
Manitowoc   (414)684-6691

Southwest Wisconsin Technical
  College*
Fennimore   (608)822-3262

University Of Wisconsin —
  Green Bay*
Green Bay   (414)465-2000

University Of Wisconsin —
  Madison*
Madison   (608)262-1234

University Of Wisconsin —
  Milwaukee
Milwaukee   (414)229-4444

University Of Wisconsin —
  Oshkosh*
Oshkosh   (414)424-1234

University Of Wisconsin — River
  Falls
River Falls   (715)425-3911

University Of Wisconsin —
  Stevens Point*
Stevens Point   (715)346-0123

University Of Wisconsin — Stout*
Menomonie   (715)232-1123

University Of Wisconsin —
  Superior*
Superior   (715)394-8101

University Of Wisconsin —
  Whitewater
Whitewater   (414)472-1234

Viterbo College*
La Crosse   (608)791-0400

Western Wisconsin Technical
  College*
La Crosse   (608)785-9200

Wisconsin Lutheran College
Milwaukee   (414)774-8620

WYOMING

Central Wyoming College*
Riverton   (307)856-9291

Eastern Wyoming College
Torrington   (307)532-7111

Western Wyoming College*
Rock Springs   (307)382-1600

*Institution indicates *comprehensive* prior learning assessment available.

Glossary

Many of the words in this glossary have two or more meanings. Here, however, they are defined in only the limited sense that is particular to their use in discussion of prior learning assessment. For instance, as a verb the word discipline can mean chastise, control, correct, punish, train; as a noun it can mean conduct, method, exercise, order, etc. In this glossary it is used only as it refers to an academic area of study.

Adult learner

One who is older than the traditional college student (25+); one who is living away from parents and/or is self-supporting; one whose primary role is other than learner (such as worker, parent, spouse, or retiree).

Articulation

The process by which students can relate what they have already learned to what they want or need to learn. Articulation can also mean relating the learnings for which they are requesting credit to their academic, personal and professional goals. Articulation is particularly useful in degree program planning.

A somewhat different meaning of articulation refers to agreements among colleges regarding the transfer of credit.

Assessment

The process of defining, documenting, measuring, evaluating and granting credit for learning acquired through experience.

Basic education

A term usually applied to work in reading, writing and mathematics designed to bring the student to an eighth- or tenth-grade level in those subjects.

CAEL

Council for Adult and Experiential Learning is an educational association dedicated to the advancement of experiential learning, fostering its valid and reliable assessment, and sponsoring research and publication on its operation and advantages. CAEL is a leader in helping adults take advantage of learning opportunities and get credit for what they know. CAEL does not itself assess individual students' learning nor award academic credit.

Certificate

A document attesting that one has completed a program and gained competency in a specific area (electronics, data processing, etc.). A certificate may entail anything from a single course to a cluster of courses and may or may not carry credit toward a degree.

CEU

Continuing education units are nontraditional education credits, usually awarded for educational experiences that are designed to meet the requirements of professional organizations. For example, teachers, nurses, physicians and accountants must earn a certain number of CEUs to maintain or enhance their professional status. Some colleges are trying to work out ways to equate CEUs to college credit, but there is as yet no widely accepted standard. Because

CEUs to date have been measures of time spent in class or workshops rather than measures of learning acquired, CAEL recommends against calibrating CEUs with college credit.

Challenge exam

An examination given by the instructor of a course to someone who wishes to get credit for the course without having taken it. Typically, the challenge exam is similar or identical to the one that the instructor gives to a class at the end of the semester.

CLEP

The College Level Examination Program is a standardized examination program offering students the opportunity to earn college credit in many common academic areas. (See also *DANTES*.)

Concentration

See *major*.

Continuing education

Courses offered on a credit or not-for-credit basis that specifically target adults, usually part-time. These courses may be offered by colleges and universities or by high schools, churches, YMCA/ YWCAs, community adult education programs, etc.

Correspondence program

A structured college syllabus or set of lessons presented in print form that offers the student an opportunity to work independently at home, reading, doing assignments and taking tests. Usually student and instructor keep in touch by mail, but some programs are using telephones and computers extensively.

Credit

The common measure of progress toward graduation in most U.S. colleges and universities. Usually one credit is granted for each class hour per week in a 1- or 16-week semester. Courses may be worth anywhere from one to five credits, with three credits being the most common. Though the numbers vary from school to school, the requirement for most associate's degrees is a total of 60 credits; for bachelors degrees, 120 credits.

Curriculum

A prescribed set of courses for an area of specialization (e.g., engineering, biology, political science).

DANTES

Defense Activity for Non-Traditional Educational Support is a standard credit by examination program offering students the opportunity to earn college credit in many common academic and technical areas. (See Appendix E.)

Degrees

College degrees are earned by completing a specified number of courses or other studies in accordance with a program design acceptable to the college or university and subject to their requirements. The common degrees are:

> Associate of arts (A.A.), associate of science (A.S.) and associate of applied science (A.A.S.) — two-year degrees, usually granted by Community Colleges.

> Bachelor of arts (B.A.), bachelor of science (B.S.), bachelor of fine arts (B.F.A.) or bachelor of professional studies (B.P.S.) — four-year degrees, granted by colleges and universities.

> Master of arts (M.A.) or master of science (M.S.) — graduate degrees, granted by universities, usually involve taking at least one full year beyond the bachelor's degree plus writing a thesis.

> Doctor of philosophy (Ph.D.) — graduate degree, granted by universities. Some people take a master's degree first. Others go right on to the Ph.D., which will then take somewhat longer. The Ph.D. coursework is usually followed by a major piece of research, called a dissertation.

Discipline

A broad field of study, such as history, psychology or computer science (as opposed to "subject," which is more specialized, such as "history of the postreconstruction period" or "adolescent psychology").

Distance learning

An expanded version of correspondence learning, distance learning offers another way for students who cannot attend classes regularly to learn though independent study, television, computers, video hookups to classes, etc. Schools with distance learning programs (see Appendix D) appeal to adults who have the ability to work well on their own. Contact with the instructor may be maintained through correspondence, phones, computers, or other electronic means.

Documentation

Evidence that supports the claim for credit for prior learning experience. Documentation may be in the form of transcripts, professional licenses or certificates, records of apprenticeships, certificates of completion of company or union training, official job descriptions, letters, news clippings or products produced by the student such as books, paintings, computer programs, hand-crafted furniture, etc.

Electives

Courses taken as part of one's degree program that are not required for the major but chosen from the school's offerings after all requirements for the major, general education or other school stipulations have been met. Well-chosen electives can round out a program, give it breadth, enable students to sample subjects in the humanities and social and physical sciences that can enrich their lives.

Evaluation

The process by which one or more faculty persons determine the credit equivalency of a specific unit of learning.

Evidence

See *documentation*.

Experiential learning

Any learning in which the learner is in direct touch with the realities being studied. This learning may be sponsored (as in work-study arrangements, internships, apprenticeships), or it may be acquired informally through hands-on experience and practice through work, travel, personal development or community service.

External degree program

An academic degree program that enables students to complete their studies without necessarily attending class. Sometimes called "colleges without walls," external degree programs are especially designed for the adult part-time learner who needs flexibility and who can work independently. (See *correspondence program* and *distance learning*.)

Faculty

Those who are responsible for teaching in colleges and universities. The common titles given to faculty, in ascending order, are lecturer, instructor, assistant professor, associate professor, and professor. In addition, schools may employ teaching assistants who are graduate students and part-time or adjunct faculty who have expertise in a specific area. A few colleges call their faculty mentors or learning facilitators, regardless of their rank.

Full-time student

One who is registered for 12 semester hours or more for credit.

G.E.D. (General Education Development)

The equivalent of a high school degree, the G.E.D. is earned through a standardized national examination that measures educational development in five areas. This exam is designed for persons who have not had the opportunity to complete the formal requirements for a high school diploma. A great many high schools and adult basic learning schools sponsor courses designed to help the adult prepare for the G.E.D. exam.

Learning component

A single, identifiable chunk of learning that is part of a larger "subject." Thus, knowledge of Pascal computer language is a learning component of computer science; knowledge of OSHA procedures is a learning component of personnel management; and understanding infant grasping behavior is a learning component of child development.

Major

The subject or discipline in which a student specializes. Using it as a noun, one can have a major in math, sociology, business studies, etc. As a verb one can major in these subjects. Each school has regulations that determine how many courses must be completed in one's major subject to fulfill the requirements of the degree.

Measurement

Ascertaining the nature of the specific learning acquired by a person — its quality, quantity and level. In most schools, measurement of learning for the purpose of prior learning assessment is done by a faculty member in the appropriate discipline or area.

Minor

In some colleges, students are required to develop a secondary area of concentration in addition to their major. For example, a political science major may have a minor in Russian language.

Part-time student

One who is registered for less than 12 hours of credit per semester.

PONSI (Program on Non-Collegiate Sponsored Instruction)

Conducted by the American Council on Education, this program evaluates courses sponsored by corporations, unions and the armed services and issues program guides that recommend credit for those deemed equivalent to college courses.

Portfolio

A document compiled by the learner in support of his or her request for credit. Although requirements may vary somewhat from school to school, the portfolio typically consists of the following sections:

> Essay — narrative that describes the learner's background and career and education goals, explains how the prior learnings were acquired, and discusses how these learnings fit into his or her proposed degree program and overall education and career plans.

Identification — description of the learnings for which the student is requesting credit, including a definition of the learning in curriculum or competency-based terms.

Articulation — explanation of how these learnings were acquired, relating them to the student's overall education and career objectives and, in some cases, to the proposed degree program.

Documentation — evidence that the learnings are valid as described.

Request for credit — list of the specific learnings for which credit is sought with numerical equivalents.

Postsecondary education

Education occurring after high school. This may include credit and noncredit courses

Practicum

A hands on experience of applying classroom learning to a real-life situation. Thus, a major in child psychology may include a practicum spent working in a child-care center.

Prerequisites

Those courses that must be completed before taking something else. Thus, beginning and intermediate Spanish may be prerequisites for Spanish literature; introduction to chemistry may be a prerequisite for nuclear chemistry.

Registrar

The college official responsible for keeping records on the enrollment and academic standing of students. The registrar also must attest to the validity of transcripts submitted for admission to advanced standing.

Resume

Although usually defined as a summary of one's work experience, for purposes of assessment the resume includes all experiences that may have resulted in learning: dates, sources, the nature of the work (or hobby or independent learning of any kind), the learnings acquired.

Semester

A period of time (usually 15 to 18 weeks) into which colleges divide the school year. Most courses last one semester and may be scheduled from two to five hours each week of that semester. There are usually two semesters in a college year, plus, in many institutions, a summer semester. Some schools have developed a *trimester* or *quarter* system, which may change both the period of time and the number of class hours (or credits) per week.

Semester hour

This is usually defined as 15 hours of class time over the course of the semester or one hour per week. Thus, a three-hour course will meet three hours per week for 15 weeks for three credits. (Most schools assume that the student also spends two hours of preparation for every hour spent in the classroom.)

Syllabus

An outline of the main points to be covered in a course. A syllabus may also include the requirements of the course or the competencies expected to be acquired as well as a list of the required textbook(s) and assignments.

Transcript

An official school document that lists the courses taken by a student, grades and credit earned, and degree awarded. The imprint of the school seal and authorized signature on the transcript attest to its validity.

Index